中等职业学校汽车运用与维修专业教学用书

汽车实用英语

（第3版）

全华科友　组织编写
赵金明　李　艳　主　　编
刘兴旺　毛　丽　副主编

人民交通出版社股份有限公司
北　京

内 容 提 要

本书是中等职业学校汽车运用与维修专业教学用书，主要内容包括：汽车基础英语、汽车维修英语、汽车应用英语，各单元末附有适量的习题。

本书可供中等职业学校汽车运用与维修专业教学使用，也可供汽车使用、维修、检测技术人员参考。

图书在版编目(CIP)数据

汽车实用英语/赵金明，李艳主编. —3版. —北京：人民交通出版社股份有限公司，2020.12
ISBN 978-7-114-16884-0

Ⅰ.①汽⋯ Ⅱ.①赵⋯ ②李⋯ Ⅲ.①汽车工程—英语—高等职业教育—教材 Ⅳ.①U46

中国版本图书馆 CIP 数据核字(2020)第194274号

书　　名：	汽车实用英语（第3版）
著 作 者：	赵金明　李　艳
责任编辑：	李　良
责任校对：	刘　芹
责任印制：	刘高彤
出版发行：	人民交通出版社股份有限公司
地　　址：	(100011)北京市朝阳区安定门外外馆斜街3号
网　　址：	http://www.ccpcl.com.cn
销售电话：	(010)59757973
总 经 销：	人民交通出版社股份有限公司发行部
经　　销：	各地新华书店
印　　刷：	北京市密东印刷有限公司
开　　本：	787×1092　1/16
印　　张：	10.75
字　　数：	221千
版　　次：	2005年6月　第1版
	2011年1月　第2版
	2020年12月　第3版
印　　次：	2022年5月　第3版　第2次印刷　累计第12次印刷
书　　号：	ISBN 978-7-114-16884-0
定　　价：	27.00元

(有印刷、装订质量问题的图书由本公司负责调换)

前 言

为深入贯彻《国务院关于加快发展现代职业教育的决定》以及教育部等六部委《关于实施职业院校制造业和现代服务业技能型紧缺人才培养培训工程的通知》精神，积极推进课程改革和教材建设，为中等职业教育教学提供更加丰富和多样化的实用教材，适应经济发展、产业升级和技术进步，满足交通运输业科学发展的需要，人民交通出版社股份有限公司和相关机构组织全国交通职业院校的专业教师，按照"专业设置与产业企业岗位需求对接、课程内容与职业标准对接、教学过程与生产过程对接、明显提升职业院校毕业生就业质量"的要求，依据教育部颁布的《中等职业院校汽车运用与维修专业领域技能型紧缺人才培养培训指导方案》，对教育部职业教育与成人教育司推荐教材进行了再版修订，供全国中等职业院校汽车运用与维修等专业教学使用。

此次再版修订教材符合国家对技能型紧缺人才培养培训工作的需要，体现了中等职业教育的特色，教材特点如下：

（1）"以服务发展为宗旨，以促进就业为导向"，加强文化基础教育，强化技术技能培养，符合初、中级汽车专业实用人才培养的需求；

（2）总结近几年教学改革经验，教材修订符合中等职业院校学生的认知规律，注重知识的实际应用和对学生职业技能的训练，符合中职院校教学与培训的需要；

（3）依据最新国家及行业标准，剔除上一版教材中陈旧过时的内容，教材修订量在20%以上，反映了新知识、新技术、新工艺。

《汽车实用英语（第3版）》是中等职业学校汽车类专业的课程用书。本书是编者在多年从事汽车构造课程教学及大量社会调研的基础上，充分考虑了目前国内中等职业教育教学的特点，紧密结合汽车新知识、新技术，在编写过程中力求将汽车基础知识与实践相结合，有较强的针对性和实用性。

全书由赵金明和北京交通运输职业学院李艳担任主编，由山东交通技师学院刘兴旺、湖南交通职业技术学院毛丽担任副主编，参与教材编写工作的还有唐山市开滦一中的李静瑜。

在本书的编写过程中，编者参考了国内外大量资料与参考文献，在此，向相关作者致以最诚挚的谢意。由于编者水平有限，书中难免有不妥和错误之处，恳请广大读者批评指正。

编 者
2020年6月

CONTENTS 目录

Unit 1 Automobile Basic English
单元 1 汽车基础英语

1.1　Car logo.. 1
　　（车标）
　　1.1.1　Do you know these car logos?.................... 1
　　　　　（你知道这些汽车标志吗？）
　　1.1.2　Do you know the original contries of these brands?............. 3
　　　　　（你知道上面这些车标是属于哪个国家的吗？）
　　1.1.3　Logo meaning（车标的含义）....................... 4
　　1.1.4　Do you know the manufacturers of these cars?....... 5
　　　　　（你知道下面几款汽车是属于哪个汽车公司吗？）
1.2　Classification of vehicles.............................. 6
　　（汽车的分类）
　　1.2.1　Automobile types................................. 6
　　　　　（汽车类型）
　　1.2.2　Cars classification by appearance................. 8
　　　　　（乘用车的分类：按车身类型分类）
　　1.2.3　Cars classification by inner space 10
　　　　　（乘用车的分类：按使用空间分类）
　　1.2.4　Cars classification by drive line................. 11
　　　　　（乘用车的分类：按驱动方式分类）
　　1.2.5　Cars classification by energy..................... 12
　　　　　（乘用车的分类：按使用能源分类）
1.3　Automotive components................................... 14
　　（汽车的组成部分）
　　1.3.1　The appearance of a car........................... 14
　　　　　（汽车外观图）

1.3.2　The center console 15
　　　（汽车内部图）
1.3.3　Dashboard and Warning light 18
　　　（仪表盘和警示灯）
1.3.4　Tools 19
　　　（随车工具）
1.3.5　Car diagrams 20
　　　（汽车图表）
1.3.6　Automobile maintenance manual 24
　　　（汽车维修手册）

Unit 2　Automobile Service English
单元2　汽车维修英语

2.1　Measuring tools 26
　　（工量具）
　2.1.1　Measurement tools in English and Chinese terminology 26
　　　（测量工具的中、英文专有名词）
　2.1.2　Hand tools in English and Chinese terminology 28
　　　（手动工具的中、英文专有名词）
　2.1.3　Power tools in English and Chinese terminology 31
　　　（动力工具的中、英文专有名词）
2.2　Five major systems of motor vehicles 34
　　（汽车的五大系统）
　2.2.1　Engine systems 34
　　　（发动机系统）
　2.2.2　Chassis system 56
　　　（底盘系统）
　2.2.3　Electrical systems 80
　　　（电气系统）
　2.2.4　Power train system 106
　　　（传动系统）
　2.2.5　Emission control systems 127
　　　（废气控制系统）

2.3　New energy automobile drive system 137
　　（新能源汽车动力系统）

Unit 3　Automobile Applied English
单元 3　汽车应用英语

3.1　Basic dialogue 145
　　（英语基本会话篇）
　　3.1.1　Customer's reception 145
　　　　　（接待顾客）
　　3.1.2　Answer terms 146
　　　　　（回答用语）
　　3.1.3　Customers reception by phone 148
　　　　　（电话接待客人）
3.2　Scene dialogue 149
　　（英语场景会话篇）
　　3.2.1　Car received calls come 149
　　　　　（来电来人购车接待）
　　3.2.2　Regular maintenance 150
　　　　　（定期维护）
　　3.2.3　How to reduce emissions 152
　　　　　（如何减少废气排放）
　　3.2.4　Traffic accident 155
　　　　　（交通事故）
　　3.2.5　The recall of automotive products 156
　　　　　（汽车产品的召回）
　　3.2.6　Car washing and waxing 158
　　　　　（洗车及打蜡）

References 161
（参考文献）

Unit 1　Automobile Basic English
单元 1　汽车基础英语

1.1　Car logo（车标）

1.1.1　Do you know these car logos?（你知道这些汽车标志吗？）

Toyota（丰田）

Honda（本田）

Volkswagen（大众）

Audi（奥迪）

Mercedes Benz（奔驰）

BMW（宝马）

Cadillac（凯迪拉克）

Jaguar（捷豹）

Lamborghini（兰博基尼）

Nissan（日产）

Buick（别克）

Mazda（马自达）

Chevrolet（雪佛兰）	Rolls-Royce（劳斯莱斯）	Geely（吉利）	Bentley（宾利）

Subaru（斯巴鲁）	Aston Martin（阿斯顿·马丁）	Lincoln（林肯）	Volvo（沃尔沃）

Ferrari（法拉利）	Ford（福特）	Great Wall Motors（长城）	Porsche（保时捷）

Morris Garages（名爵）	Opel（欧宝）	Suzuki（铃木）	Jinbei Auto（金杯）

Bugatti（布加迪）	Dodge（道奇）	FIAT（菲亚特）	Peugeot（标致）

Roewe（荣威）	Renault（雷诺）	SAAB（萨博）	Chery（奇瑞）

| Mitsubishi（三菱） | Tesla（特斯拉） | Land Rover（路虎） |

| KIA（起亚） | Chrysler（克莱斯勒） | Citroen（雪铁龙） |

1.1.2　Do you know the original contries of these brands?
（你知道上面这些车标是属于哪个国家的吗？）

China _____

USA _____

Japan _____

British _____

French _____

Germany _____

Italy _____

1.1.3 Logo meaning（车标的含义）

Toyota：丰田（日本）

丰田车标是由两个椭圆形组成的左右对称结构。两个椭圆表示汽车制造者与顾客心心相印。上下相交的两个椭圆组合在一起，形成丰田（Toyota）的第一个字母T。空白处表示Toyota的先进技术在世界范围内拓展延伸，面向未来，面向宇宙不断飞翔，表现公司具有日益进步的技术水平及无穷的创新机会。

BMW：宝马（德国）

宝马汽车公司初创是生产航空发动机的，标志上的蓝色代表天空，白色代表螺旋桨，为蓝白相间的对称图形与公司所在地巴伐利亚州的州徽相同。

Geely：吉利（中国）

车标含义：吉利的标志为勋章/盾牌形状，由六块宝石组成，蓝色宝石代表蔚蓝的天空，黑色宝石寓意广阔的大地，双色宝石的组合象征吉利汽车驰骋天地之间，走遍世界的每个角落。

Mercedes Benz：奔驰（德国）

奔驰的三角星分别代表陆地、海洋和天空，表示其无论在海上、天空还是陆地都能神通广大。

Audi：奥迪（德国）

奥迪汽车的标志为四个圆环，代表着合并前的四家公司。最初设在萨克森州的四家汽车公司——茨维考市（Zwickau）的奥迪（Audi）和霍希（Horch）汽车公司、开姆尼-西格玛市（Chemnitz-Siegmar）的漫游者汽车公司（Wanderer）以及Zschopau市的DKW汽车公司，对当时德国汽车工业的进步做出了杰出的贡献。这四家汽车公司于1932年合并为汽车联盟股份公司（Auto Union AG，以下简称汽车联盟）。就汽车产量来说，汽车联盟是当时德国第二大汽车制造公司，商品标志为四个连接的圆环，代表参与合并的四家汽车公司。

Lamborghini：兰博基尼（意大利）

公司的标志是一头浑身充满了力量，正准备向对手发动猛烈攻击的斗牛。据说兰博基尼本人就具有这种不甘示弱的牛脾气，体现了兰博基尼公司产品的特点，因为公司生产的汽车都是大功率、高性能的运动型轿车。车头和车尾上的商标去掉了公司名，只剩下一头斗牛。

1.1.4 Do you know the manufacturers of these cars?
（你知道下面几款汽车是属于哪个汽车公司吗？）

a. Toyota

b. BMW

c. Nissan

d. General Motors

e. Volkswagen

1.2 Classification of vehicles（汽车的分类）

1.2.1 Automobile types（汽车类型）

Fire engine 消防车

Police car 警车

Car 小汽车

Sport Utility Vehicle (SUV) 运动型多用途车

Tow truck 拖车

Agricultural vehicle 农用汽车

Concrete mixer 搅拌车

Truck 货车

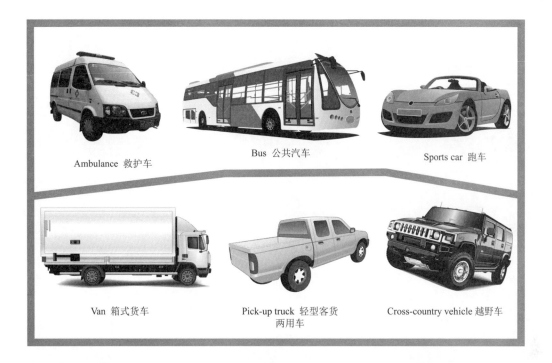

Functional exercises(功能性练习)

1. Please translate into English.(请翻译成英文)

❶ 消防车 _____
❷ 警车 _____
❸ 救护车 _____
❹ 拖车 _____
❺ 搅拌车 _____

2. Please translate into Chinese.(请翻译成中文)

❶ truck _____
❷ bus _____
❸ SUV _____
❹ pick-up truck _____
❺ sports car _____

1.2.2 Cars classification by appearance
（乘用车的分类：按车身类型分类）

Sedan
轿车
　　轿车是乘用车的基本型。从廉价的紧凑型车到高级豪华车，这种车型的应用范围非常广泛。

Coupe
双门跑车
　　追求驾驶乐趣的运动型跑车。比三厢车高度更低，一般设有两个车门。

Hatchback car
掀背车
　　车体后部设有向上开启的车门。这种车型正逐步成为小型车的主流。

Station wagon
旅行车
　　旅行车为两厢车，其行李舱和驾驶室连为一体，提高了存放货物的能力。

Pickup truck
轻型客货两用车
　　车室前方有独立的发动机舱，后方带有敞开式货车车厢，是货车的一种。

Sport Utility Vehicle（SUV）
运动型多用途车
　　可越野行驶，结构坚固，乘坐舒适的乘用车。是从小型敞篷车进化出的车型。

Minivan
厢式旅行车
　　两厢车的一种。有3排座席和行李空间。属于车内空间宽敞的家庭用车。

Minibus
中型客车
　　发动机舱上为驾驶室。基本上与单厢车同义。

Convertible
敞篷车
　　车篷为开闭式或装卸式。又称为"Cabriolet"（篷式汽车）。

Multi Purpose Vehicle
MPV（多用途车）
　　MPV是从旅行轿车逐渐演变而来的，一般为多厢式结构，强调多功能性，是集轿车、旅行车和商务车于一身的车型。

Bus
公交车
　　指在城市道路上循固定路线，承载旅客出行的机动车辆。一般外形为方形，有窗，设置座位。

英语语法（English grammar）：

数词（Numbers）

　　在英语的学习当中，数词是非常重要的。数词是表示数目和顺序的词。表示数目的词叫基数词，表示顺序的词叫序数词。

基数词		序数词	
1, 2, 3, 4, 5, 6, 7, 8, 9, 10, 11, 12	one, two, three, four, five, six, seven, eight, nine, ten, eleven twelve	第一 第二 第三	first (1st), second (2nd), third (3rd) 口诀：第一、第二、第三是特殊
13, 14, 15, 16, 17, 18, 19	thirteen, fourteen, fifteen, sixteen, seventeen, eighteen, nineteen 口诀：十几是在几后面"+" teen	第四	fourth(4th)
		第五	fifth(5th)
		第六	sixth(6th)
21, 22, 23, 24, 25, 26, 27, 28, 29	twenty-one, twenty-two, twenty-three, twenty-four, twenty-five, twenty-six, twenty-seven, twenty-eight, twenty-nine 口诀：几十几是在相应的几十（ty）后面"+"上几	第七	seventh(7th)
		第八	eighth(8th)
		第九	ninth(9th)
		第十	tenth(10th)
		第十一	eleventh(11th)
		第十二	twelfth(12th)
20, 30, 40, 50, 60, 70, 80, 90	twenty, thirty, forty, fifty, sixty seventy, eighty, ninety 口诀：几十是"+" ty	第十三	thirteenth(13th)
		第十四	fourteenth(14th)
		第十五	fifteenth(15th)
		第十六	sixteenth(16th)
100, 1,000, 10,000, 1,000,000	hundred, thousand, ten thousand, million 口诀：上了百就是hundred，上了千就是thousand，上了万就是ten thousand，上了百万就是million	第十七	seventeenth(17th)
		第十八	eighteenth(18th)
		第十九	nineteenth(19th)
		第二十	twentieth(20th)

1.2.3 Cars classification by inner space
（乘用车的分类：按使用空间分类）

One Box Car 单厢车

车身为一个厢体的乘用车称为单厢车。发动机舱设在驾驶席的下面，同驾驶室一体化。车内空间宽敞，可存放多件行李物品，商用车多采用这种设计。

Two Box Car 两厢车

发动机舱和驾驶室分开的乘用车。在车辆发生正面碰撞时安全性很高，货物存放空间也很大。结合了单厢车和三厢车的优点。

Three Box Car 三厢车

发动机舱、驾驶室、行李舱分别独立存在的乘用车。从侧面看，像是3个车厢连在一起。这是乘用车最普通的外形。在发生碰撞时，发动机舱、行李舱可以起到缓冲作用，因而安全性能比较高。

- Car 最初用于日常会话，只是表示一辆车的意思，并没有摩托车、货车和公交车的意思，一般指小汽车特别是小型乘用车。
- Vehicle 主要是运送手段和乘坐工具的总称，自行车、电车、拖拉机等都包含在其中，汽车一般是指road vehicles，是在道路上奔跑的交通工具。
- Automobile 是汽车的正式说法，汽车的通称。

1.2.4 Cars classification by drive line
（乘用车的分类：按驱动方式分类）

FF方式

FF是front engine front drive的缩写。意思是前置发动机和变速器，前轮驱动。发动机和驱动系统集中在一处，有效利用了空间。发动机一般横置，不过也有纵置发动机的FF车。

优点：

采用FF方式可使车内空间变大，因此小型车和厢式旅行车多采用此设计。在冰雪等湿滑路面上，比采用FR方式设计的车辆更具有安全性。近几年，三厢车中采取这种方式也逐渐成为主流。

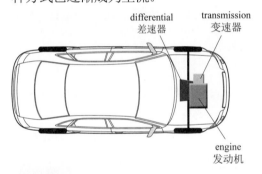

FR方式

FR是front engine rear drive的缩写。意思是前部纵置发动机、后轮驱动。车厢下部必须安装将动力传到后轮的传动轴。车体质量比前后约为1∶1，达到完美的质量平衡。

优点：

采用FR方式的车体，具有很好的质量平衡，转弯设定的自由度很高。不过因为部件很多，成本有所提高，所以这种采用这种方式的汽车多为高级车或跑车。

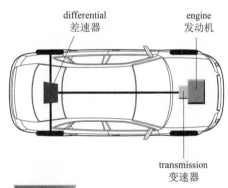

MR方式

MR是middle engine rear drive的缩写。意思是车厢和后轮车轴之间安置发动机，后轮驱动。在乘用车中很少使用这种方式。

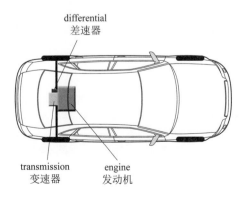

RR方式

RR是rear engine rear drive的缩写。意思是发动机和变速器安置在后轮车轴的后方。同MR方式一样，在乘用车中使用RR方式的情况很少。

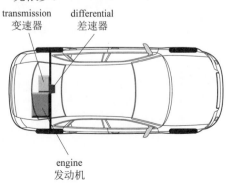

FF方式和FR方式有什么差异？

一直以来，在乘用车中采用后轮驱动的FR方式占据主流地位。这是因为，前轮同时安装传动系和转向系时运转不是很平稳，结合处的性能也很低。不过通过技术改进后，现在即使是FF方式，车辆也可进行平稳的行驶，而且通过提高装置的性能，减小其占用空间，也有空间剩余来充当行李舱。在这方面，将以前普遍的纵置发动机改为横置发动机具有很大的影响。

FF方式的性能不比FR方式的逊色，FF方式以车内空间宽大的优势引起顾客的注意，而且在易滑路面比FR方式更加安全，因而采用FF方式的车种发展迅速。现在，FF方式在逐渐被小型车、中型车采用。

尽管如此，FR方式也并不是完全没有自身的优势。在车辆起动时，后轮驱动的加速性能更好。而且采用FR方式，车辆转向更方便。因此，现在高档轿车中很少采用FF方式，均为FR方式。

1.2.5 Cars classification by energy
（乘用车的分类：按使用能源分类）

Fuel vehicle： 燃油车，主要有汽油车(Gasoline vehicle)和柴油车(Diesel vehicle)。

Gas vehicle： 燃气车，主要有液化石油气车LPG (Liquefied Petroleum Gas)和压缩天然气车CNG(Compressed Natural Gas)。

Electric vehicle： 电动车，主要有纯电动汽车BEV (Blade Electric Vehicle)、混合动力汽车HEV(Hybrid Electrical Vehicle)、燃料电池汽车FCEV(Fuel Cell Electric Vehicle)。

通常，燃油车被称为传统动力汽车，不全部采用燃油作为动力来源，而采用新型车载动力装置和清洁能源的汽车，都称为新能源汽车。除了我们所熟知的纯电动、混合动力汽车外，新能源汽车还包括燃气车、氢能源车、太阳能电池汽车等。随着环保意识的增强，新能源汽车被越来越多的人所接受。

★ Practice makes perfect（熟能生巧）

1. Match（对应）

_____ (1) FF   A. 后置后驱

_____ (2) FR   B. 汽车

_____ (3) CNG   C. 中置后驱

_____ (4) LPG   D. 车辆

_____ (5) RR   E. 小汽车

_____ (6) MR   F. 运动型多用途车

_____ (7) car   G. 液化石油气

_____ (8) automobile   H. 前置后驱

_____ (9) vehicle   I. 压缩天然气

_____ (10) SUV   J. 前置前驱

2. Choice（选择）

_____ (1) There are many_____in Beijing.
      A. the taxi   B. taxi
      C. a taxi   D. taxies

_____ (2) The shuttle bus can carry a lot of _____.
      A. passenger   B. passengers
      C. a passenger   D. the passenger

_____ (3) What's wrong_____your car?
      A. with   B. for
      C. to   D. at

_____ (4) Which type of car is nonpolluting to the environment?
      A. CNG and LPG   B. oil
      C. diesel   D. petrol

_____ (5) Which car is dedicated for hospital?
      A. ambulance   B. police car
      C. tractor   D. crane car

1.3 Automotive components（汽车的组成部分）

1.3.1 The appearance of a car（汽车外观图）

1.3.2 The center console（汽车内部图）

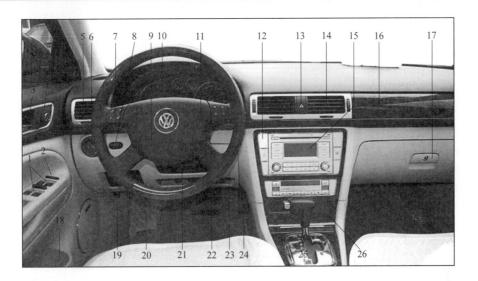

编号	英文	中文
1	electrical window lifter switch	电动车窗玻璃升降器开关
2	center control lock button	中央集控门锁按钮
3	internal spanner	内开扳手
4	rearview mirror regulator tap	后视镜调节开关
5	vent	出风口
6	light switch	灯光开关
7	turn indicator, dimming lever and cruise control system switch	转向信号灯、变光拨杆和巡航控制系统开关
8	dashboard lighting control rotary knob	仪表盘照明调节旋钮
9	air bag	安全气囊
10	clustered instrument board	组合式仪表盘
11	horn button	喇叭按钮
12	rear window heater switch	后窗玻璃加热装置开关

续上表

编 号	英 文	中 文
13	hazard warning light switch	危险警告灯开关
14	vent	出风口
15	radio	收音机
16	copilot air bag	副驾驶席安全气囊
17	storage tank	储藏箱
18	cup shelf	杯架
19	engine cap unlock mechanism	发动机舱盖开锁装置
20	clutch pedal	离合器踏板
21	controlling shaft	转向盘高度调节操纵杆
22	brake pedal	制动踏板
23	certificates and book storage tank	随车证件和书籍储藏箱
24	accelerate pedal	加速踏板
25	gear lever	换挡杆
26	car cigarette lighter	附带有点烟器/插座的烟灰盒

Unit 1 Automobile Basic English
单元1 汽车基础英语

★ **Practice makes perfect**（熟能生巧）

  1. Look at the picture and fill in the blanks（看图填空）

❶（　　　　）　　❷（　　　　）　　❸（　　　　）

❹（　　　　）　　❺（　　　　）　　❻（　　　　）

❼（　　　　）　　❽（　　　　）　　❾（　　　　）

❿（　　　　）　　⓫（　　　　）　　⓬（　　　　）

2. Please translate into English（请翻译成英文）

加速踏板 ＿＿＿＿＿＿＿＿　　　发动机舱 ＿＿＿＿＿＿＿＿

制动踏板 ＿＿＿＿＿＿＿＿　　　门锁 ＿＿＿＿＿＿＿＿

前照灯 ＿＿＿＿＿＿＿＿　　　座椅 ＿＿＿＿＿＿＿＿

行李舱 ＿＿＿＿＿＿＿＿　　　空调 ＿＿＿＿＿＿＿＿

刮水器 ＿＿＿＿＿＿＿＿　　　喇叭 ＿＿＿＿＿＿＿＿

1.3.3 Dashboard and Warning light
（仪表盘和警示灯）

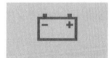
Generator
（发电机）

Preheater
（预热装置）

Airbag system
（安全气囊系统）

ESP electronic stability control system, traffic
（ESP 电控行车稳定系统）

Trailer turn signal device
（拖车转向信号装置）

Adjustable air suspension system
（可调空气悬架系统）

Adjustable air suspension system
（可调空气悬架系统）

Emission monitoring system
（尾气监控系统）

Engine power electronic control system
（发动机功率电子控制系统）

Turn signal device (left turn signal)
转向信号装置
（左转向信号灯）

Turn signal device (Right turn signal)
转向信号装置
（右转向信号灯）

Seat belt warning light
（安全带警告灯）

High beam
（远光灯）

Cruise device
（定速巡航装置）

ABS
（防抱死制动系统）

Parking brake
（驻车制动器）

Brake failure
（制动装置故障）

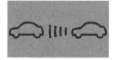
Driving with the car
（跟车行驶）

No car driving in front
（前方无车时的行驶）

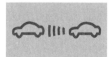
Require drivers to take over the driving
（要求驾驶人接管驾驶）

Malfunction indicator lamp/Brake light damage
（灯泡故障指示灯/制动灯损坏）

Excessive wear of brake linings
（制动摩擦片磨损过度）

Automotive batteries
（汽车蓄电池电量）

Malfunction indicator lamp/Bulb damage
（灯泡故障指示灯/灯泡损坏）

Check the engine oily bits
（检查发动机油油位）

Engine oil sensor damage
（发动机机油传感器损坏）

Fuel stock is too low
（燃油不足）

Cleaning fluid level is too low
（清洗液液位过低）

High key is not in the car!
（高级钥匙不在汽车中！）

Light and rain sensor damage
（光线及雨量传感器损坏）

Diesel engine particulate filter plug
（柴油发动机颗粒滤清器堵塞）

Dynamic headlight range adjustment lighting failure
（动态前照灯照明距离调节故障）

Wireless remote control key in the battery
（无线遥控钥匙电池）

Adaptive light damage
（自适应车灯损坏）

Ignition switch failure
（点火开关故障）

Damage to the glass window wiper
（车窗玻璃刮水器损坏）

1.3.4 Tools（随车工具）

Jack（千斤顶）　　Tire pressure（胎压计）　　Fire extinguisher（灭火器）

Tire（轮胎）　　Wire rope（钢丝绳）　　Battery line（蓄电池线）

1.3.5　Car diagrams（汽车图表）

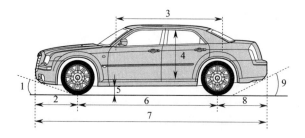

编号	英文	中文
1	front overhang angle	接近角
2	front overhang	前悬
3	length of body	车厢长度
4	height of body	车厢高度
5	ground clearance	离地间隙
6	wheel space	轴距
7	total lenght	总长度
8	rear overhang	后悬
9	rear overhang angle	离去角

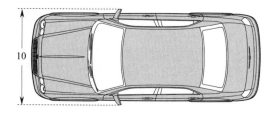

10	total width	总宽度

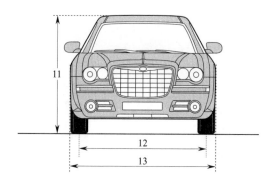

11	total height	总高度
12	track width	轮距
13	width of body	车厢宽度

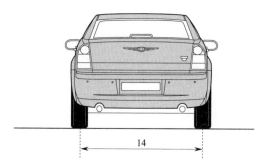

14	track width	轮距

Example of a Vehicle Specification Chart （车辆规格参数表示例）

Model (型号)	PASSAT (1.8T)	PASSAT (2.0)
■ Dimension and Weight（尺寸及质量）		
Total Lenght(全长)，mm	4780	4780
Total Width(全宽)，mm	1740	1740
Total Height(全高)，mm	1470	1470
Horsepower(马力)	150	115
Oil Capacity(机油容量)，L	4.5	4.5
Trunk volume(行李舱容积)，L	475	475
Wheelbase(轴距)，mm	2803	2803
Track Width(Front)【轮距（前）】，mm	1498	1498
Track Width(Rear)【轮距（后）】，mm	1500	1500
Minimum Ground Clearance【最小离地间隙（空载）】，mm	105	105
Complete Vehicle Kerb Mass（整备质量），kg	1420	1425
Specification of Tire(Front)【轮胎规格（前）】	195/65r15	195/65r15
Specification of Tire(Rear)【轮胎规格（后）】	195/65r15	195/65r15
■ Engine（发动机）		
Cylinders（汽缸数）	4个	4个
Capacity（排气量），mL	1781	1984
Maximum Power（最大功率），kW	110/5700r/min	85/5400r/min
Maximum Torque（最大转矩），N·m	210/1700r/min	172/3500r/min
Bore×Travel Stroke（缸径及行程），mm×mm	81×86.4	82.5×92.8
Compression Ratio（压缩比）	9.3	10.3
Full Speed（最高车速），km/h	208	182
Fuel Delivery Equipment（燃油供给装置）	多点电喷	多点电喷
Type of Gear Box（变速器类型）	MT	AT
Tank Capacity（油箱容积），L	62	62
Fule Consumption of 100km（百公里油耗），L/100km	7.3	8.0
■ Braking System/Suspension System/Drive Line（制动系统/悬架/驱动方式）		
Braking System (Front/Rear)【制动系统（前/后）】	通风盘	通风盘
Suspension System (Front)【悬架系统（前）】	多连杆式独立悬架	多连杆式独立悬架
Suspension System (Rear)【悬架系统（后）】	纵向托臂式扭力梁	纵向托臂式扭力梁
Drive Line（驱动方式）	前置前驱	前置前驱

★ **Practice makes perfect**（熟能生巧）

 1. Look at the picture and fill in the blacks（看图填空）

❶    ❷   ❸

_____   _____   _____

❹    ❺   ❻

_____   _____   _____

 2. Match（对应）

_____ (1) tail-lights   A. 自动变速器

_____ (2) wheel   B. 后视镜

_____ (3) adjustable seats   C. 刮水器

_____ (4) headlight   D. 转速表

_____ (5) tachometer   E. 仪表盘

_____ (6) wiper   F. 前照灯

_____ (7) dashboard   G. 转向盘

_____ (8) rear mirror   H. 可调节座椅

_____ (9) automatic transmission   I. 车轮

_____ (10) steering wheel   J. 尾灯

3. Translator（翻译）

Please translate into Chinese（请翻译成中文）

(1) accelerate pedal　_____

(2) horn button　_____

(3) sun visor　_____

(4) map light　_____

(5) cigar lighter　_____

(6) storage pocket　_____

(7) floor mat　_____

(8) cup holder　_____

(9) sunroof　_____

(10) turning light　_____

Please translate into English（请翻译成英文）

(1) 制动灯　_____

(2) 雾灯　_____

(3) 安全带　_____

(4) 行李舱　_____

(5) 前翼子板　_____

(6) 顶灯　_____

(7) 臂枕　_____

(8) 安全头枕　_____

(9) 门锁　_____

(10) 扩音器　_____

1.3.6　Automobile maintenance manual（汽车维修手册）

■ **Query index**（查询索引）

Taking the use of Toyota Yaris maintenance manual as an example, we inquire about the information of engine oil. We find the information about motor oil on page LU-1.

1NZ - FE ENGINE MECHANICAL - ENGINE　　　　　　　　EM-1

ENGINE

ON-VEHICLE INSPECTION

1. **INSPECT ENGINE COOLANT (See page CO-1)**
2. **INSPECT ENGINE OIL (See page LU-1)**
3. **INSPECT BATTERY (See page CH-4)**
4. **INSPECT AIR CLEANER FILTER ELEMENT SUB-ASSEMBLY**
   (a) Remove the air cleaner filter element sub-assembly.
   (b) Visually check that there is no dirt, blockage, or damage to the air cleaner filter element.
   HINT:
   - If there is any dirt or a blockage in the air cleaner filter element, clean it with compressed air.
   - If any dirt or a blockage remains even after cleaning the air cleaner filler element with compressed air, replace it.
5. **INSPECT SPARK PLUG (See page IG-5)**
6. **INSPECT IGNITION TIMING**
   (a) When using an intelligent tester:
   　(1) Warm up and stop the engine.
   　(2) Connect the intelligent tester to the DLC3.
   　(3) Turn the ignition switch ON.
   　(4) Select the following menu items:
   　　DIAGNOSIS / ENHANCED OBD II/ ACTIVE TEST / TC (TE1) / ON.
   　　HINT:
   　　Refer to the intelligent tester operator's manual for further details.
   　(5) Inspect the ignition timing during idling.
   　　Ignition timing:
   　　　8 to 12 degrees BTDC
   　　NOTICE:
   　　- Turn all the electrical systems and the A/ C off.
   　　- Inspect the ignition timing with the cooling fan off.
   　　- When checking the ignition timing, shift the transmission to the neutral position.
   　(6) Select the following menu items: TC (TE1) / OFF.
   　(7) Turn the ignition switch OFF.
   　(8) Disconnect the intelligent tester from the DLC3.
   (b) When not using an intelligent tester:
   　(1) Remove cylinder head cover No 2 (see page IG-9).

EM

Access to information（查阅资料）

We found the information of engine oil according to the page number. We could find what we need through these informations.

1NZ - FE LUBRICATION - LUBRICATION SYSTEM   LU-1

LUBRICATION SYSTEM
ON-VEHICLE INSPECTION

1. CHECK ENGINE OIL LEVEL
   (a) Warm up the engine, then stop the engine and wait for 5 minutes. Check that the engine oil level is between the low and full marks on the oil level gauge.
   If the engine oil level is low, check for oil leakage and add engine oil up to the full level mark.
   NOTICE:
   Do not add engine oil to above the full level mark.

2. CHECK ENGINE OIL QUALITY
   (a) Check the oil for deterioration, water intrusion, discoloration and thinning.
   Oil grade:
   Use IL5AC multigrade engine oil.
   5AE 5W-30 is the best choice for good fuel economy and good starting in cold weather.

Recommended Viscosity (SAE):

5W-30

| °F | −20 | 0 | 20 | 40 | 60 | 80 | 100 |
| °C | −29 | −19 | −7 | 4 | 16 | 27 | 38 |

TEMPERATURE RANGE ANTICIPATED BEFORE NEXT OIL CHANGE

3. REMOVE ENGINE OIL PRESSURE SWITCH ASSEMBLY
   (a) Remove the engine under cover LH.
   (b) Remove the engine under cover RH.
   (c) Disconnect the engine oil pressure switch assembly connector

Unit 2　Automobile Service English
单元 2　汽车维修英语

2.1　Measuring tools（工量具）

2.1.1　Measurement tools in English and Chinese terminology（测量工具的中、英文专有名词）

1. Ruler or Steel scale（钢尺），Fig.2-1.

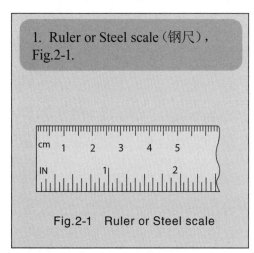

Fig.2-1　Ruler or Steel scale

2. Thickness gauge（厚薄规），Fig.2-2.

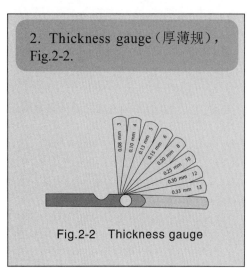

Fig.2-2　Thickness gauge

3. Wire gauge（线径规），Fig.2-3.

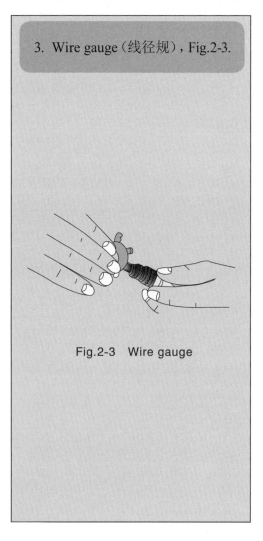

Fig.2-3　Wire gauge

4. Micrometer（千分尺）
(1) Inside micrometer（内径千分尺），Fig.2-4.

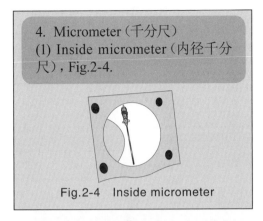

Fig.2-4　Inside micrometer

6. Cylinder-bore gauge（量缸表），Fig.2-7.

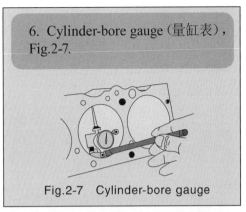

Fig.2-7　Cylinder-bore gauge

(2) Outside micrometer（外径千分尺），Fig.2-5.

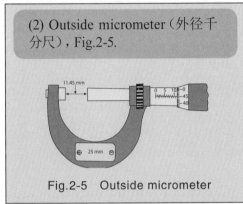

Fig.2-5　Outside micrometer

7. Depth gauge（深度规），Fig.2-8.

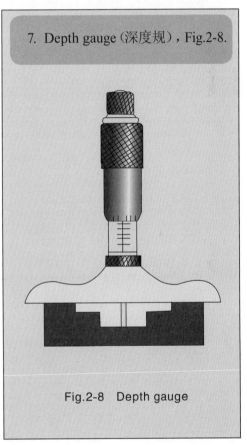

Fig.2-8　Depth gauge

5. Dial gauge（百分表），Fig.2-6.

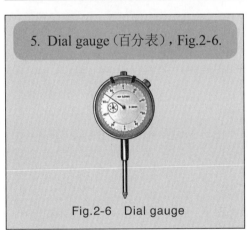

Fig.2-6　Dial gauge

8. Vernier caliper（游标卡尺），Fig.2-9.

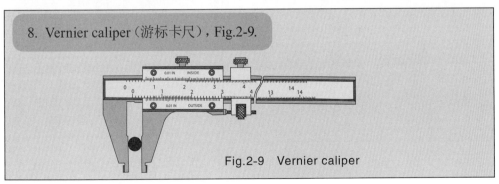

Fig.2-9　Vernier caliper

2.1.2 Hand tools in English and Chinese terminology
（手动工具的中、英文专有名词）

1. Striking tools（敲击工具）

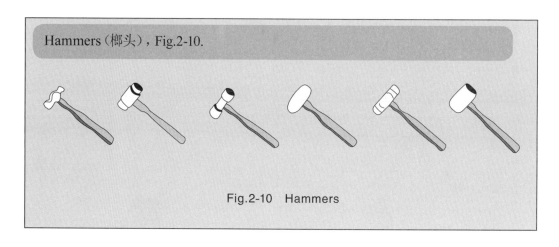

Hammers（榔头），Fig.2-10.

Fig.2-10 Hammers

2. Turning tools（转动工具）

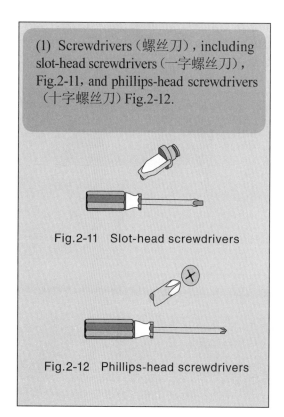

(1) Screwdrivers（螺丝刀），including slot-head screwdrivers（一字螺丝刀），Fig.2-11, and phillips-head screwdrivers（十字螺丝刀）Fig.2-12.

Fig.2-11 Slot-head screwdrivers

Fig.2-12 Phillips-head screwdrivers

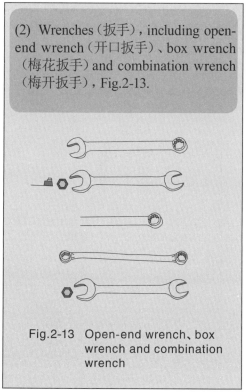

(2) Wrenches（扳手），including open-end wrench（开口扳手）、box wrench（梅花扳手）and combination wrench（梅开扳手），Fig.2-13.

Fig.2-13 Open-end wrench、box wrench and combination wrench

(3) Flare-nut wrench(油管扳手), Fig.2-14.

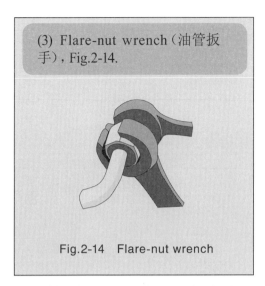

Fig.2-14　Flare-nut wrench

(4) Adjustable wrench(活动扳手), Fig.2-15.

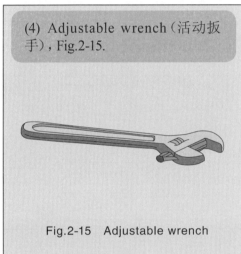

Fig.2-15　Adjustable wrench

(5) Torque wrench(扭力扳手), Fig.2-16.

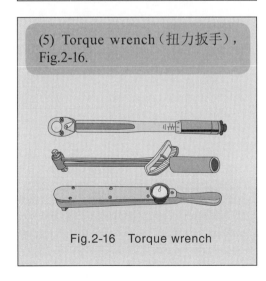

Fig.2-16　Torque wrench

3. gripping tools(夹持工具)

(1) Gripping pliers(夹持钳), Fig.2-17.

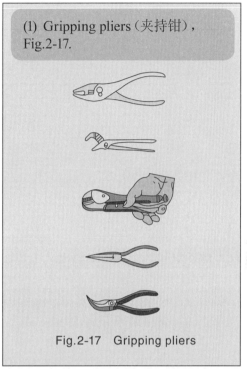

Fig.2-17　Gripping pliers

(2) Cutting pliers(剪切钳), Fig.2-18.

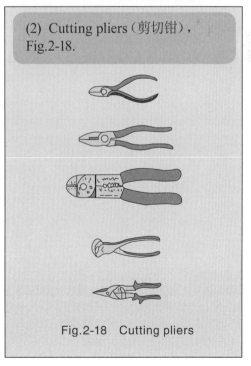

Fig.2-18　Cutting pliers

(3) Stud extractor(螺桩拔取器), Fig.2-19.

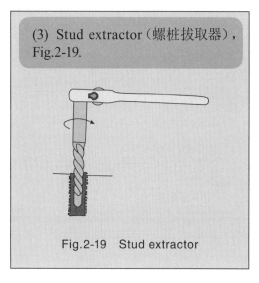

Fig.2-19 Stud extractor

(3) Hacksaw(手弓锯), Fig.2-22.

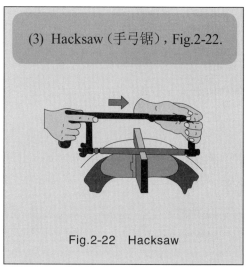

Fig.2-22 Hacksaw

4. Cutting tools(切削工具)

(1) Chisels(凿刀), Fig.2-20.

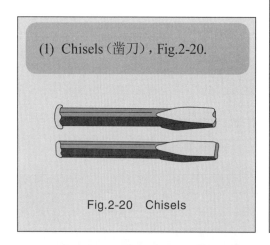

Fig.2-20 Chisels

(4) Punches(冲销), Fig.2-23.

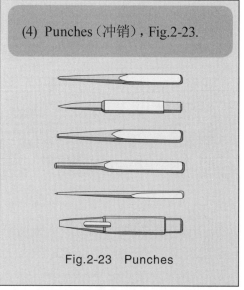

Fig.2-23 Punches

(2) Files(锉刀), Fig.2-21.

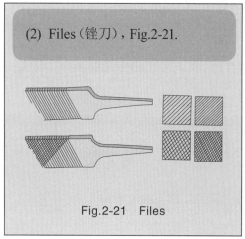

Fig.2-21 Files

(5) Tubing cutter(切管器), Fig.2-24.

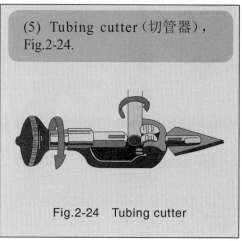

Fig.2-24 Tubing cutter

2.1.3 Power tools in English and Chinese terminology
（动力工具的中、英文专有名词）

1. Electric tools（电动工具）

(1) Electric drill（电钻），Fig.2-25.

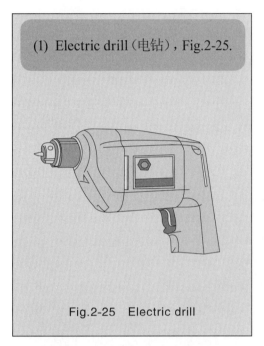

Fig.2-25　Electric drill

(2) Grinder（砂轮机），Fig.2-26.

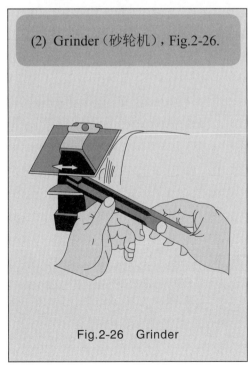

Fig.2-26　Grinder

(3) Soldering gun（电烙铁），Fig.2-27.

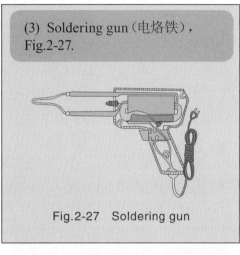

Fig.2-27　Soldering gun

(4) Drill press（钻床），Fig.2-28.

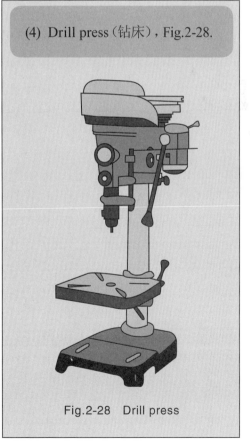

Fig.2-28　Drill press

2. Pneumatic tools（气动工具）

(1) Air hammer（气动冲击器）, Fig.2-29.

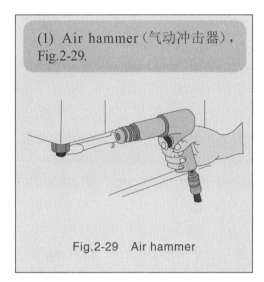

Fig.2-29 Air hammer

(2) Air impact wrench（气动冲击扳手）, Fig.2-30.

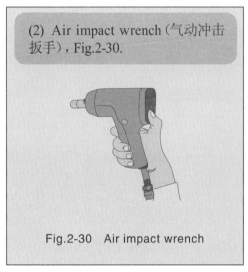

Fig.2-30 Air impact wrench

(3) Air ratchet（气动棘轮扳手）, Fig.2-31.

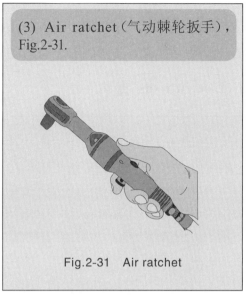

Fig.2-31 Air ratchet

(4) Pneumatic jacks（气动千斤顶）, Fig.2-32.

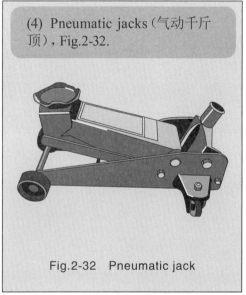

Fig.2-32 Pneumatic jack

(5) Air drill（气动钻头）, Fig.2-33.

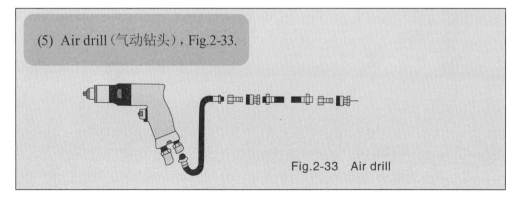

Fig.2-33 Air drill

3. hydraulic tools(液压工具)

(1) Hydraulic jack(液压千斤顶), Fig.2-34.

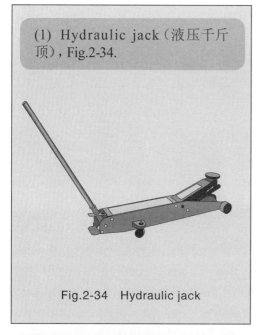

Fig.2-34　Hydraulic jack

(3) Hydraulic press(液压压床), Fig.2-36.

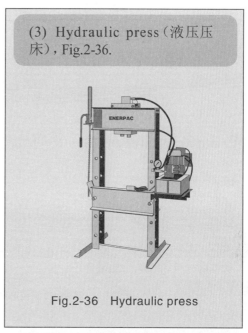

Fig.2-36　Hydraulic press

(2) Shop crane(吊车), Fig.2-35.

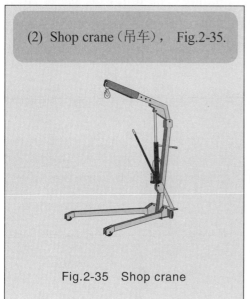

Fig.2-35　Shop crane

(4) Lifter(举升机), Fig.2-37.

Fig.2-37　Lifter

2.2 Five major systems of motor vehicles（汽车的五大系统）

2.2.1 Engine systems（发动机系统）

1 Basic engine parts（发动机的基本零件）

Vocabulary

engine ['endʒin]	n.	发动机
provide [prə'vaid]	v.	提供
power ['pauə(r)]	n.	动力
wheel [wi:l]	n.	车轮
vehicle ['vi:əkl]	n.	车辆
automobile ['ɔ:təməbi:l]	n.	汽车
gasoline ['gæsəli:n]	n.	汽油
diesel ['di:zl]	n.	柴油
combustion [kəm'bʌstʃən]	n.	燃烧
energy ['enədʒi]	n.	能量
process [prə'ses]	n.	过程
mixture ['mikstʃə(r)]	n.	混合物
cylinder head ['silində(r) hed]	n.	汽缸盖
cylinder block ['silində blɔk]	n.	汽缸体
seal [si:l]	v.	密封
valve [vælv]	n.	气门
spark plug [spɑ:k plʌg]	n.	火花塞
rocker arm ['rɔkə(r) ɑ:m]	n.	摇臂
chamber ['tʃeimbə(r)]	n.	室
camshaft ['kæmʃɑ:ft]	n.	凸轮轴
crankshaft ['kræŋkʃɑ:ft]	n.	曲轴

1) Engine parts

The engine provides the power to drive the wheels of the vehicle. All automobile engines, both gasoline and diesel, are classified as internal combustion engines because the combustion or burning that creates energy takes place inside the engine. The combustion process is the burning of the air-fuel mixture. The following pages cover the basic parts and the major systems of a one-cylinder engine. Shown in Fig.2-38.

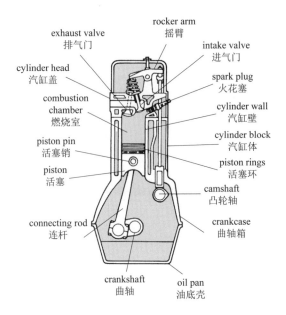

Fig.2-38　Engine parts

2) Cylinder head

The cylinder head fits on top of the cylinder block to close off and seal the top of the cylinder. It also holds the camshaft and valves, the spark plugs and the rocker arms. The combustion chamber is a small volume between the bottom of the cylinder head and the top of the piston. It is an area into which the air-fuel mixture is compressed and burned. Shown in Fig.2-39.

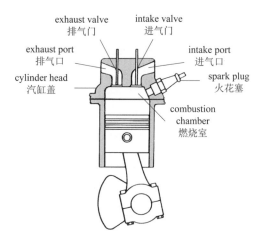

Fig.2-39　Cylinder head

3) Cylinder block

The biggest part of the engine is the cylinder block, which is also called engine block. It is a large casting of metal, that is drilled with holes for the passage of lubricant and coolant, provide spaces for movement of mechanical parts. The block contains the cylinders, which are round passageways fitted with pistons. The block houses or holds the major mechanical parts of the engine. Shown in Fig.2-40.

4) Valve train

A valve train is a series of parts used to open and close the intake and exhaust ports. A valve is a movable part that opens and closes a passageway. A camshaft controls the movement of the valves, causing them to open and close at the proper time. Springs are used to help close the valves. Shown in Fig.2-41.

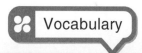

Vocabulary

engine block　　　n. 发动机缸体
['endʒin blɔk]
lubricant ['lu:brikənt]　n. 润滑剂
coolant ['ku:lənt]　　n. 冷却液
cylinder ['silində(r)]　n. 汽缸
passageway ['pæsidʒwei] n. 通道
piston ['pistən]　　　n. 活塞
valve train [vælv trein] n. 气门机构
intake ['inteik]　　　n. 进气
exhaust [iɡ'zɔ:st]　　n. 排气
port [pɔ:t]　　　　　n. 端口
movement ['mu:vmənt]　n. 动作
proper ['prɔpə(r)]　　adj. 适当的
spring [spriŋ]　　　n. 弹簧

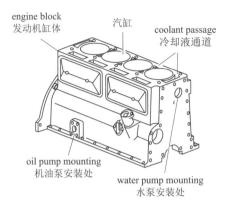
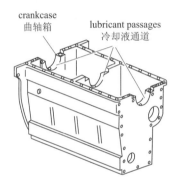

Fig.2-40　Cylinder block

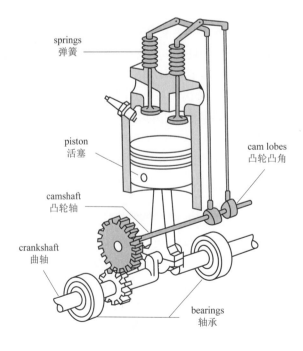

Fig.2-41　Valve train

★ Practice makes perfect（熟能生巧）

1. Match（对应）

_____ (1) engine   A. 车辆
_____ (2) vehicle   B. 汽缸体
_____ (3) gasoline   C. 凸轮轴
_____ (4) cylinder head   D. 汽缸
_____ (5) cylinder block E. 活塞
_____ (6) camshaft   F. 弹簧
_____ (7) spark plug   G. 发动机
_____ (8) rocker arm   H. 汽缸盖
_____ (9) engine block   I. 润滑剂
_____ (10) cylinder   J. 气门机构
_____ (11) piston   K. 排气
_____ (12) lubricant   L. 发动机缸体
_____ (13) valve train   M. 火花塞
_____ (14) exhaust   N. 汽油
_____ (15) spring   O. 摇臂

2. Choice（选择）

_____ (1) Which of these can provide the power?
   A. valve train
   B. cylinder block
   C. cylinder head
   D. engine

_____ (2) Which of these can seal the top of the cylinder?
   A. automobile
   B. camshaft
   C. spark plug
   D. cylinder head

_____ (3) The camshaft and valves are held by the:
  A. cylinder block
  B. cylinder head
  C. spark plug
  D. chamber

_____ (4) A camshaft controls the movement of the:
  A. valves
  B. spark plug
  C. chamber
  D. piston

3. Translation（翻译）

(1) The engine provides the power to drive the wheels of the vehicle.

_____

(2) The cylinder head fits on top of the cylinder block to close off and seal the top of the cylinder.

_____

(3) The biggest part of the engine is the cylinder block, which is also called engine block.

_____

(4) A valve train is a series of parts used to open and close the intake and exhaust ports.

_____

2 Four-stroke cycle engine (四冲程发动机)

1) Intake stroke

The first stroke of the cycle is the intake stroke. As the piston moves away from top dead center (TDC), the intake valve opens. The downward movement of the piston increases the volume of the cylinder above it, causing the atmospheric pressure to push a mixture of air and fuel through the open intake valve. The intake valve closes after the piston has reached bottom dead center (BDC). Shown in Fig.2-42.

2) Compression stroke

The compression stroke begins as the piston starts to move from BDC. The intake valve and the exhaust valve closes, trapping the air-fuel mixture in the cylinder. The upward movement of the piston compresses the air-fuel mixture, thus heating it up. At TDC, the piston head and the cylinder head form the combustion chamber in which the fuel will be burned. Shown in Fig.2-43.

Vocabulary

stroke [strəuk]	n. 行程
cycle ['saikl]	n. 循环
downward ['daunwəd]	adj. 向下的
atmospheric [ˌætməs'ferik]	adj. 大气的
pressure ['preʃə(r)]	n. 压力
push [puʃ]	v. 推动
reach [riːtʃ]	v. 到达
bottom ['bɔtəm]	n. 底部
compression [kəm'preʃən]	n. 压缩
trap [træp]	v. 堵塞
upward ['ʌpwəd]	adj. 向上的
form [fɔːm]	v. 形成

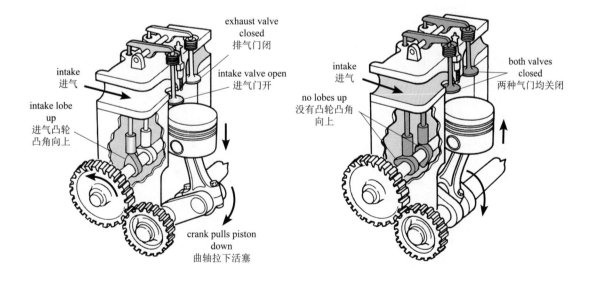

Fig.2-42　Intake stroke　　　　Fig.2-43　Compression stroke

Vocabulary

ignite [ig'nait]	v. 点燃
electrical [i'lektrikl]	adj. 电气的
electrode [i'lektrəud]	n. 电极
expand [ik'spænd]	v. 膨胀
transmit [træns'mit]	v. 传送
connecting rod [kə'nektiŋ rɔd]	n. 连杆
crankshaft ['kræŋkʃɑ:ft]	n. 曲轴
reach [ri:tʃ]	v. 到达
cause [kɔ:z]	v. 致使
rush [rʌʃ]	v. 催逼
remaining [ri'meiniŋ]	adj. 剩余的
complete [kəm'pli:t]	v. 完成

3) Power stroke

The power stroke begins as the compressed air-fuel mixture being ignited. An electrical spark across the electrodes of a spark plug ignites the air-fuel mixture. The burning fuel rapidly expands, creating a very high pressure against the top of the piston. This drives the piston down toward BDC. The power of the piston downward movement is transmitted through the connecting rod to the crankshaft. Shown in Fig.2-44.

4) Exhaust stroke

The exhaust valve opens just before the piston reaches BDC on the power stroke. Pressure within the cylinder causes the exhaust gas to rush through the open valve and into the exhaust system. The piston back from BDC pushes away most of the remaining exhaust gas from the cylinder. As the piston reaches nearby TDC, the exhaust valve begins to close as the intake valve starts to open. The exhaust stroke completes the four-stroke cycle. Shown in Fig.2-45.

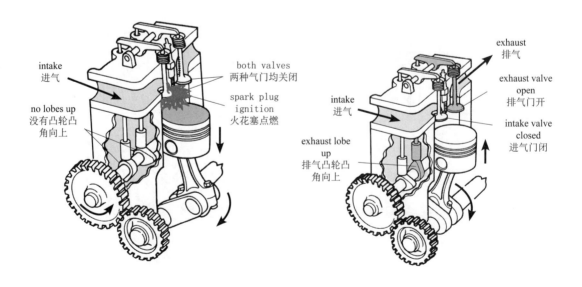

Fig.2-44　Power stroke　　　　　　Fig.2-45　Exhaust stroke

★ Practice makes perfect （熟能生巧）

1. Match（对应）

_____ (1) stroke   A. 膨胀

_____ (2) cycle   B. 向上的

_____ (3) downward   C. 电气的

_____ (4) compression   D. 电极

_____ (5) upward   E. 大气的

_____ (6) pressure   F. 行程

_____ (7) bottom   G. 曲轴

_____ (8) ignite   H. 循环

_____ (9) electrical   I. 向下的

_____ (10) electrode   J. 剩余的

_____ (11) expand   K. 连杆

_____ (12) remaining   L. 底部

_____ (13) connecting rod   M. 压缩

_____ (14) crankshaft   N. 压力

_____ (15) atmospheric   O. 点燃

2. Choice（选择）

_____ (1) Which of these is the first stroke of the four-stroke cycle engine?

        A. intake stroke

        B. compression stroke

        C. power stroke

        D. exhaust stroke

_____ (2) Which of these can ignite the compressed air-fuel mixture?

        A. coolant

        B. camshaft

        C. spark plug

        D. valve

(3) The power of piston downward movement is transmitted through the connecting rod to the:
   A. camshaft
   B. crankshaft
   C. electrode
   D. chamber

(4) When does the intake stroke finish?
   A. the piston moves away from TDC
   B. the piston moves away from BDC
   C. the compressed air-fuel mixture is ignited
   D. the exhaust valve opens

3. Translation（翻译）

(1) As the piston moves away from top dead center (TDC), the intake valve opens.

_____

(2) The cylinder head fits on top of the cylinder block to close off and seal the top of the cylinder.

_____

(3) The piston making upward movement compresses the air-fuel mixture, thus heating it up.

_____

(4) As the piston reaches nearby TDC, the exhaust valve begins to close as the intake valve starts to open.

_____

3 Fuel system（燃油系统）

1) Function of fuel system

The fuel system is designed to supply the correct amount of fuel mixed with the correct amount of air to the cylinders of the engine. It is made up of several different parts. As shown in Fig.2-46, a fuel tank stores the fuel. Fuel pump moves the fuel from the fuel tank to the engine. Fuel injectors or a carburetor mix the fuel up with air for delivery to the cylinders. There are three basic types of automotive fuel systems: carburetor, gasoline and diesel injection systems.

Vocabulary

system ['sistəm]	n. 系统
supply [sə'plai]	v. 提供
amount [ə'maunt]	n. 数量
fuel tank ['fjuːəl tæŋk]	n. 油箱
store [stɔː(r)]	v. 储存
fuel pump ['fjuːəl pʌmp]	n. 燃油泵
injector [in'dʒektə]	n. 喷油器
carburetor [ˌkɑːbə'retə(r)]	n. 化油器
delivery [di'livəri]	n. 输送
injection [in'dʒekʃn]	n. 喷射

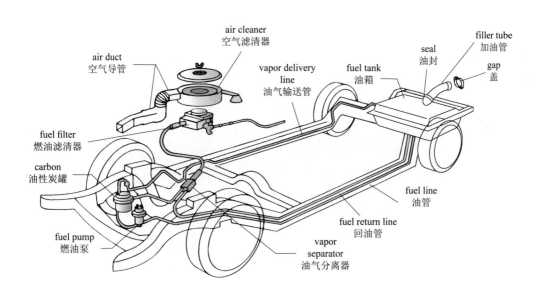

Fig.2-46 Function of fuel system

Vocabulary

measure	['meʒə(r)]	v. 测量
sensor	['sensə(r)]	n. 传感器
manifold	['mænifəuld]	n. 歧管
vacuum	['vækjuəm]	n. 真空
convert	[kən'və:t]	v. 转换
process	[prə'ses]	v. 处理
calculate	['kælkjuleit]	v. 计算
signal	['signəl]	n. 信号

2) Gasoline injection system

The engine fuel are measured by intake airflow passing a sensor or by intake manifold pressure. As shown in Fig.2-47. The airflow or manifold vacuum sensor converts its reading to an electrical signal and sends it to the engine control computer. The computer processes this signal (and others) and calculates the fuel needs of the engine. The computer then sends an electrical signal to the fuel injector or injectors.

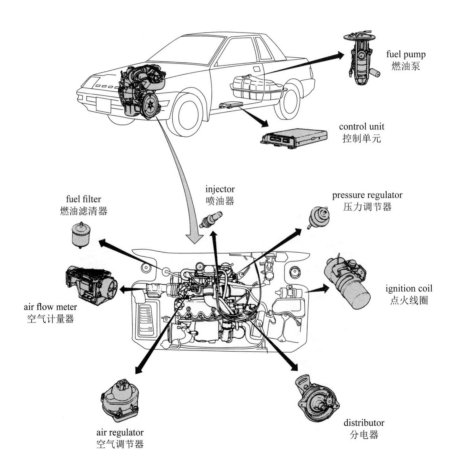

Fig.2-47 Gasoline injection system

3) Diesel fuel system

The diesel fuel injection system contains the following components: (1) Fuel tank and pick-up unit; (2) Fuel line; (3) Fuel pump system; (4) Fuel filter; (5) Water-in-fuel sensor (some systems); (6) Water-in-fuel separator (some systems); (7) Fuel heater (some systems); (8) Injection nozzles. The supply pump draws the fuel from the fuel tank and delivers it to the distributor pump housing. The injection pump then increases the fuel pressure to the levels needed for combustion. The governor controls the speed of the engine. Shown in Fig.2-48.

Vocabulary	
filter ['fɪltə(r)]	n. 滤清器
separator ['sepəreitə]	n. 分离器
heater ['hi:tə(r)]	n. 加热器
nozzle ['nɒzl]	n. 喷油嘴
draw [drɔ:]	v. 吸取
distributor pump [di'strɪbjutə(r) pʌmp]	n. 分配泵
governor ['gʌvənə(r)]	n. 调速器

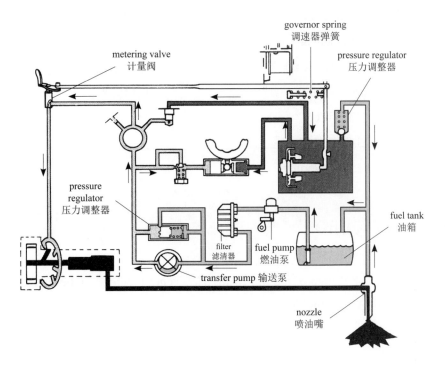

Fig.2-48　Diesel fuel system

★ Practice makes perfect（熟能生巧）

1. Match（对应）

_____ (1) fuel tank   A. 喷油器
_____ (2) fuel pump   B. 计量
_____ (3) injector   C. 雾化
_____ (4) carburetor   D. 滤清器
_____ (5) metering   E. 歧管
_____ (6) atomization   F. 真空
_____ (7) vaporization   G. 油箱
_____ (8) idle   H. 燃油泵
_____ (9) accelerator   I. 蒸发
_____ (10) sensor   J. 喷油嘴
_____ (11) manifold   K. 怠速的
_____ (12) vacuum   L. 传感器
_____ (13) filter   M. 加速器
_____ (14) nozzle   N. 化油器
_____ (15) governor   O. 调速器

2. Choice（选择）

_____ (1) Which of the following parts is not included in the fuel system?
   A. fuel tank
   B. fuel pump
   C. cylinder head
   D. fuel injector

_____ (2) The carburetor is used to mix fuel with:
   A. air
   B. coolant
   C. lubricant
   D. gasoline

_____ (3) Modern gasoline injection systems use a computer and sensors to determine the amount of fuel required. The engine fuel needs are measured by intake air flow passing a sensor or by:
    A. intake manifold temperature
    B. exhaust manifold temperature
    C. exhaust manifold pressure
    D. intake manifold pressure

_____ (4) Which of these can control the speed of the diesel engine?
    A. sensor
    B. distributor pump
    C. governor
    D. signal

3. Translation（翻译）

(1) There are three basic types of automotive fuel systems: carburetor, gasoline and diesel injection systems.

_____

(2) There are six basic carburetor circuits: float, idle, main metering, full power, accelerator pump and choke.

_____

(3) The engine fuel needs are measured by intake airflow passing a sensor or by intake manifold pressure.

_____

(4) The supply pump draws the fuel from the fuel tank and delivers it to the distributor pump housing.

_____

4 Cooling system（冷却系统）

Vocabulary

cooling system ['ku:liŋ 'sistəm]	n. 冷却系统
circulate ['sə:kjəleit]	v. 循环
comprise [kəm'praiz]	v. 包含
water jacket ['wɔ:tə(r) 'dʒækit]	n. 水套
radiator ['reidieitə(r)]	n. 散热器
cap [kæp]	n. 盖子
thermostat ['θə:məstæt]	n. 节温器
fan [fæn]	n. 风扇
hose [həuz]	n. 管子
pulley ['puli]	n. 滑轮；皮带轮
allow [ə'lau]	v. 允许
spot [spɔt]	n. 点
maximum ['mæksiməm]	adj. 最大的

1) Functions and parts of the cooling system

If the engine is maintained at a constant temperature, it will run more efficiently. The most common way to cool an engine is to circulate a liquid coolant through passages in the engine block and cylinder head. The cooling system comprises: the water pump, the water jacket, the radiator, the expansion tank, the pressure cap, the thermostat, the cooling fan and the hoses. As shown in Fig.2-49.

2) Water pump and water jacket

The heart of the cooling system is the water pump. Its job is to move the coolant through the cooling system, shown in Fig.2-50. Typically, the water pump is driven by the crankshaft through pulleys and a drive V-belt. Water jackets are designed to allow coolant to flow to the right spots so that maximum cooling can be obtained.

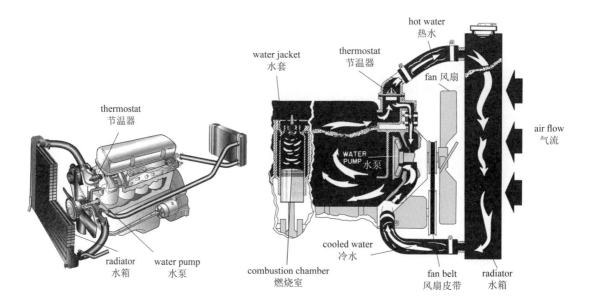

Fig.2-49 Cooling system

Fig.2-50 Water pump and water jacket

3) Radiator and expansion tank

The purpose of the radiator is to allow fresh air to reduce the temperature of the coolant. This causes a transfer of heat from the hot coolant to the cooler air. The expansion tank is designed to hold any coolant that passes through the pressure cap when the engine is hot. Shown in Fig.2-51.

4) Pressure cap and thermostat

Pressure cap is placed on the radiator. It is designed to: (1) Increase the pressure on the cooling system; (2) Reduce cavitation; (3) Protect the radiator hoses; (4) Prevent or reduce surging. As shown in Fig.2-52. The thermostat is used to bring the coolant temperature up to operating temperature as quick as possible. It is operated by a wax pellet. Common thermostats are designed to open at 82 °C and 90 °C.

Vocabulary

expansion	[ik'spænʃn]	n. 膨胀
purpose	['pə:pəs]	n. 目的
reduce	[ri'dju:s]	v. 降低
transfer	[træns'fə:(r)]	v. 传送
increase	[in'kri:s]	v. 增加
cavitation	[ˌkævi'teiʃən]	n. 空穴作用
prevent	[pri'vent]	v. 避免
surge	[sə:dʒ]	v. 波动
wax	[wæks]	n. 蜡
pellet	['pelit]	n. 丸

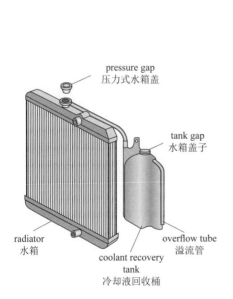

Fig.2-51 Radiator and expansion tank

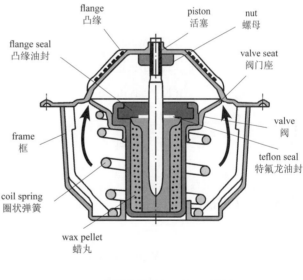

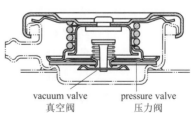

Fig.2-52 Pressure cap and thermostat

★ Practice makes perfect（熟能生巧）

1. Match（对应）

_____ (1) cooling system   A. 水套
_____ (2) efficiently   B. 散热器
_____ (3) circulate   C. 风扇
_____ (4) water jacket   D. 管子
_____ (5) fan   E. 盖子
_____ (6) cap   F. 有效率地
_____ (7) thermostat   G. 新鲜空气
_____ (8) radiator   H. 丸
_____ (9) hose   I. 冷却系统
_____ (10) pulley   J. 空穴作用
_____ (11) spot   K. 蜡
_____ (12) fresh air   L. 循环
_____ (13) cavitation   M. 节温器
_____ (14) wax   N. 点
_____ (15) pellet   O. 皮带轮

2. Choice（选择）

_____ (1) Which of the following parts is not included in the cooling system?
　　　　A. water pump
　　　　B. water jacket
　　　　C. thermostat
　　　　D. piston

_____ (2) Which is the heart of the cooling system?
　　　　A. water jacket
　　　　B. thermostat
　　　　C. cooling fan
　　　　D. water pump

_____ (3) Pressure cap is placed on:
   A. the water pump
   B. the radiator
   C. the water jacket
   D. the cooling fan

_____ (4) Which of these statements about the cooling fan is wrong?
   A. pressure cap is designed to increase the pressure
   B. the expansion tank is designed to hold the coolant
   C. typically, the water pump is driven by the crankshaft
   D. the cooling fan is designed to allow the coolant to flow to the right spots

3. Translation（翻译）

(1) The most common way to cool an engine is to circulate a liquid coolant through passages in the engine block and cylinder head.

_____

(2) Typically, the water pump is driven by the crankshaft through pulleys and a drive V-belt.

_____

(3) The expansion tank is designed to hold any coolant that passes through the pressure cap when the engine is hot.

_____

(4) The thermostat is used to bring the coolant temperature up to operating temperature as quick as possible.

_____

5 Lubrication system（润滑系统）

Vocabulary

lubrication [ˌluːbrɪˈkeɪʃən]	n.	润滑
limit [ˈlɪmɪt]	v.	限制
friction [ˈfrɪkʃn]	n.	摩擦
oil pan [ɔɪl pæn]	n.	油底壳
gallery [ˈɡæləri]	n.	油道
regulator [ˈreɡjuleɪtə(r)]	n.	调整器
distribute [dɪˈstrɪbjuːt]	v.	分配
throughout [θruːˈaʊt]	prep.	遍及
rotor [ˈrəʊtə(r)]	n.	转子
gear [ɡɪə(r)]	n.	齿轮
displacement [dɪsˈpleɪsmənt]	n.	排量
revolution [ˌrevəˈluːʃn]	n.	旋转
shaft [ʃɑːft]	n.	轴

1) Purpose of the lubrication system

The moving parts of an engine need constant lubrication. Lubrication limits the amount of wear and reduces the amount of friction in the engine. The main components of the system are the oil pan, oil pump, main oil galleries, oil filters, oil pressure regulators, oil coolers and oil sensors. Fig.2-53 shows the lubrication system.

2) Oil pump

For the oil to be distributed throughout the engine, it must be pressurized. This is done with an oil pump. The oil pump is located in the crankcase place so that oil can be drawn from the oil pan and sent into the engine. The most commonly used oil pumps are the rotor and gear types. Both are positive displacement pumps. That is, a fixed volume of oil passes through the pump with each revolution of its drive shaft. Oil pump is show in Fig.2-54.

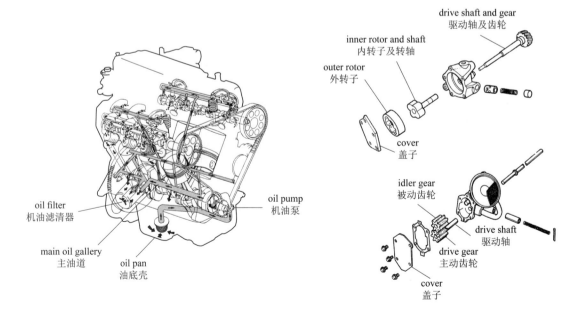

Fig.2-53 Purpose of the lubrication system

Fig.2-54 Oil pump

3) Oil pressure regulating valve and oil filter

The faster an oil pump turns, the greater its output pressure becomes. Whenever the oil pressure exceeds the maximum pressure, the regulator valve opens to reduce the pressure. All of the oil that leaves the oil pump is directed to the oil filter. This ensures that very small particles of dirt and metal carried by the oil will not reach the close-fitting engine parts. As shown in Fig.2-55.

4) Oil sensor and oil gauge

Oil pressure sensors are used to indicate if the oil system has the right amount of pressure. Fig.2-56 shows how an electrical oil pressure gauge works. As oil pressure is sensed from the main oil gallery, it changes the resistance of the circuit. This change in resistance causes the oil pressure gauge to be read differently for different pressures.

Vocabulary

exceed [ik'si:d]	v. 超过
ensure [in'ʃuə(r)]	v. 确保
particle ['pɑ:tikl]	n. 微粒
dirt [də:t]	n. 污物
metal ['metl]	n. 金属
close-fitting [kləus 'fitiŋ]	adj. 紧密配合的
gauge [geidʒ]	n. 油表
indicate ['indikeit]	v. 指示
resistance [ri'zistəns]	n. 电阻
circuit ['sə:kit]	n. 电路

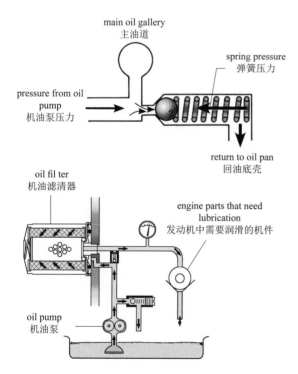
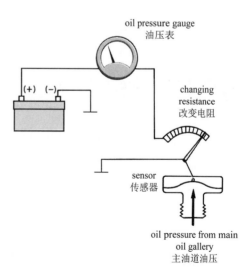

Fig.2-55 Oil pressure regulating valve and oil filter   Fig.2-56 Oil sensor and oil gauge

★ Practice makes perfect（熟能生巧）

1. Match（对应）

_____ (1) lubrication   A. 油底壳

_____ (2) friction   B. 油道

_____ (3) oil pan   C. 齿轮

_____ (4) gallery   D. 排量

_____ (5) crankcase   E. 微粒

_____ (6) rotor   F. 污物

_____ (7) gear   G. 紧密配合的

_____ (8) displacement   H. 电阻

_____ (9) regulator   I. 电路

_____ (10) shaft   J. 摩擦

_____ (11) particle   K. 润滑

_____ (12) dirt   L. 转子

_____ (13) close-fitting   M. 曲轴箱

_____ (14) resistance   N. 轴

_____ (15) circuit   O. 调整器

2. Choice（选择）

_____ (1) The moving parts of an engine need constant:

        A. lubrication

        B. air

        C. gasoline

        D. friction

_____ (2) Which of these can pressurize the oil?

        A. oil pan

        B. oil pump

        C. gallery

        D. regulator

_____ (3) Which of these can sense the oil pressure?

        A. oil gauge

        B. oil filter

        C. oil pressure sensor

        D. oil pump

_____ (4) Which of these statements about the lubrication system is wrong?

        A. oil pressure sensors are used to indicate the oil pressure

        B. you can read the oil pressure from an oil gauge

        C. the coolant can reduce the amount of friction in the engine

        D. the most commonly used oil pumps are the rotor and gear types

3. Translation (翻译)

(1) Lubrication limits the amount of wear and reduces the amount of friction in the engine.

_____

(2) The most commonly used oil pumps are the rotor and gear types.

_____

(3) Whenever the oil pressure exceeds the maximum pressure, the regulator valve opens to reduce the pressure.

_____

(4) Oil pressure sensors are used to indicate if the oil system has the right amount of pressure.

_____

2.2.2 Chassis system（底盘系统）

1 Steering system（转向系统）

Vocabulary

steering	['stiəriŋ]	n. 转向
front	[frʌnt]	adj. 前面的
rear	[riə(r)]	adj. 后面的
linkage	['liŋkidʒ]	n. 连杆
manual	['mænjuəl]	adj. 手动的
column	['kɔləm]	n. 柱
suspension	[sə'spenʃn]	n. 悬架
brake	[breik]	v. 制动
rack	[ræk]	n. 齿条
pinion	['pinjən]	n. 小齿轮
rotate	[rəu'teit]	v. 旋转
housing	['hauziŋ]	n. 外壳
lighter	['laitə(r)]	adj. 较轻的
practical	['præktikl]	adj. 实用的

1) Steering system function and parts

The purpose of the steering system is to turn the front wheels, as shown in Fig.2-57. In some cases, it also turns the rear wheels. The steering system is composed of three major sub-systems: the steering linkage, manual steering gear, and steering column and wheel. The steering system always works together with the suspension and braking systems to allow drivers to control a car.

2) The rack and pinion steering system

Rack and pinion steering system consists of a flat gear (the rack) and a small pinion gear, shown in Fig.2-58. When the steering wheel rotates the pinion gear, causes the rack to move left or right in the housing. This motion moves the remaining steering linkage to turn the front wheels. This system is lighter in weight and very practical for small cars.

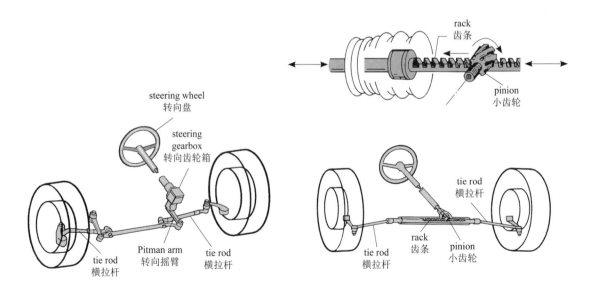

Fig.2-57　Steering system　　　Fig.2-58　The rack and pinion steering system

3) The recirculating ball steering system

The recirculating ball steering system is generally found in large cars. Fig.2-59 shows the system. As the steering wheel is rotated, the worm shaft rotates, causing the ball nut to move up or down the worm shaft. The movement of the nut causes the sector shaft to rotate and swing the pitman arm. The Pitman arm then connects to the tie rod to turn the wheels.

4) The power steering system

The power steering system is designed to reduce the amount of effort required to turn the steering wheel. Power steering systems are grouped into two types: conventional and electronically controlled. In the conventional arrangement, hydraulic power is used to assist the driver. The system shown in Fig.2-60.

Vocabulary

recirculating ball [ri:'sə:kjuleitiŋ bɔ:l]	n. 循环滚珠	
generally ['dʒenərəli]	adv. 通常	
worm shaft [wə:mʃɑ:ft]	n. 蜗杆	
nut [nʌt]	n. 螺母	
sector ['sektə(r)]	n. 扇形齿	
swing [swiŋ]	v. 摆动	
Pitman arm ['pitmən ɑ:m]	n. 转向摇臂	
tie rod [tai rɔd]	n. 横拉杆	
power steering	n. 动力转向装置	
effort ['efət]	n. 力量	
require [ri'kwaiə(r)]	v. 要求	
group [gru:p]	v. 区分	
conventional [kən'venʃənl]	adj. 传统式的	
hydraulic [hai'drɔ:lik]	adj. 液压的	
assist [ə'sist]	v. 协助	

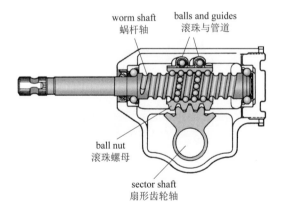

Fig.2-59 The recirculating ball steering system

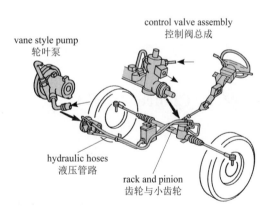

Fig.2-60 The power steering system

★ Practice makes perfect（熟能生巧）

1. Match（对应）

_____ (1) steering   A. 小齿轮
_____ (2) rack   B. 手动的
_____ (3) pinion   C. 转向
_____ (4) linkage   D. 液压的
_____ (5) manual   E. 齿条
_____ (6) suspension   F. 外壳
_____ (7) brake   G. 后面的
_____ (8) hydraulic   H. 动力转向装置
_____ (9) housing   I. 柱
_____ (10) tie rod   J. 循环滚珠
_____ (11) rear   K. 实用的
_____ (12) practical   L. 制动
_____ (13) column   M. 横拉杆
_____ (14) recirculating ball   N. 连杆
_____ (15) power steering   O. 悬架

2. Choice（选择）

_____ (1) What is the purpose of the steering system?
    A. to turn the front wheels
    B. to turn on the lights
    C. to circulate the coolant
    D. to stop a vehicle

_____ (2) Which of the following parts is not included in the recirculating ball steering system?
    A. worm shaft   B. ball nut
    C. sector   D. rack gear

_____ (3) Which of the following statements about the rack and pinion steering system is true?

    A. It is lighter in weight

    B. It is heavier in weight

    C. It is generally found in larger cars

    D. It uses hydraulic power to assist the driver

_____ (4) The recirculating ball steering system is used. When the steering wheel rotates, the ball nut moves:

    A. up or down

    B. left or right

    C. forth and back

    D. inside and outside

3. Translation（翻译）

(1) The purpose of the steering system is to turn the front wheels.

(2) Rack and pinion steering consists of a flat gear (the rack) and a small pinion gear.

(3) The recirculating ball steering system is generally found in large cars.

(4) Power steering systems are grouped into two types: conventional and electronically controlled.

2 Wheel alignment(车轮校正)

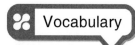 Vocabulary

alignment [ə'lainmənt]	n. 校正
pavement ['peivmənt]	n. 柏油路
scuff [skʌf]	v. 拖行
drag [dræg]	v. 拖曳
slip [slip]	v. 偏滑
strain [strein]	n. 过度疲劳;滥用
stability [stə'biləti]	n. 稳定性
tire ['taiə(r)]	n. 轮胎
safety ['seifti]	n. 安全

1) Purpose of wheel alignment

Wheel alignment is a check of how the wheels contact the pavement, as shown in Fig.2-61. The main purpose of wheel alignment is to allow the wheels to roll without scuffing, dragging, or slipping on the road. Good alignment results in:

① Better fuel economy

② Less strain on the front-end parts

③ Directional stability

④ Easier steering

⑤ Longer tire life

⑥ Increased safety

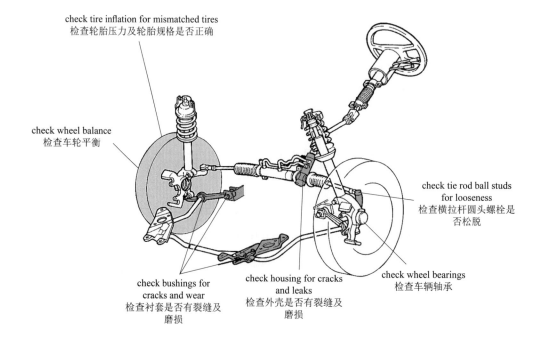

Fig.2-61　Purpose of wheel alignment

2) Caster

On a steered wheel, caster is the angle between the spindle axis and the vertical line, as viewed from the side. Backward tilt is called positive caster. Caster is designed to provide steering stability. It is the first angle adjusted during an alignment. The caster angle for each wheel on an axle should be equal. Shown in Fig.2-62.

3) Camber

Camber is defined as the inward or outward tilt of the wheels on a vehicle, as viewed from the front or rear side. Camber is measured as an angle in degrees from the center line of the wheel to a true vertical line. As shown in Fig.2-63. The purpose of checking camber is to make sure the tire is vertical to the road. Shown in Fig.2-63.

Vocabulary

caster ['kɑːstə(r)]	n. 主销后倾角
spindle ['spindl]	n. 心轴
axis ['æksis]	n. 轴线
vertical ['vəːtikl]	adj. 垂直的
backward ['bækwəd]	adj. 向后的
tilt [tilt]	n. 倾斜
adjust [ə'dʒʌst]	v. 调整
axle ['æksl]	n. 轴
camber ['kæmbə(r)]	n. 外倾角
inward ['inwəd]	adj. 向内的
outward ['autwəd]	adj. 向外的
degree [di'griː]	n. 度

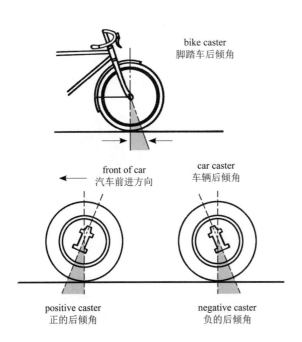

Fig.2-62　Caster

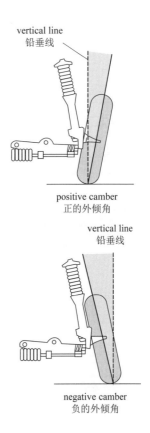

Fig.2-63　Camber

Vocabulary

inclination [ˌinkliˈneiʃn]	n. 内倾
angle [ˈæŋgl]	n. 角度
pivot [ˈpivət]	n. 枢轴
straight ahead [streit əˈhed]	n. 直线前进
included angle [inˈklu:did ˈæŋgl]	n. 包容角
toe [təu]	n. 轴踵
difference [ˈdifrəns]	n. 差别
toe-in [təu in]	n. 前束
toe-out [təu aut]	n. 前展
critical [ˈkritikl]	adj. 关键的
excessively [ikˈsesivli]	adv. 非常地

4) Steering axis inclination (SAI)

The SAI is the angle between the true vertical line and a line drawn between the steering pivots as viewed from the front of the vehicle. It helps the vehicles steering system return to straight ahead after a turn. Shown in Fig.2-64. When the camber angle is added to the SAI angle, the sum of the two is called the included angle.

5) Toe in

Toe is defined as the difference in the distance between the front and back of the front wheels. Fig.2-65a) shows the toe. If the leading edge distance is less, then there is toe-in. If it is greater, there is toe-out. Actually, toe is critical as a tire-wearing angle. Incorrect toe adjustment will cause the tires to wear excessively and will cause harder steering.

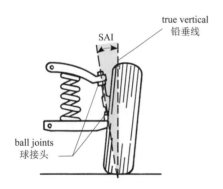

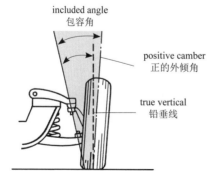

Fig.2-64 Sai

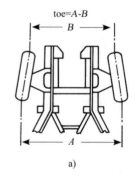

a)

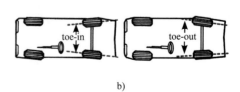

b)

Fig.2-65 Toe in

6) Thrust angle

When the steering wheel is in the straight-ahead position, if rear toe does not parallel the vehicle centerline, a thrust direction to the left or right is created. This difference of rear toe from the geometric centerline is called the thrust angle. As shown in Fig.2-66.

Vocabulary		
thrust [θrʌst]		n. 推力
parallel ['pærəlel]		v. 平行
centerline ['sentəlain]		n. 中心线
geometric [ˌdʒi:ə'metrik]		adj. 几何的

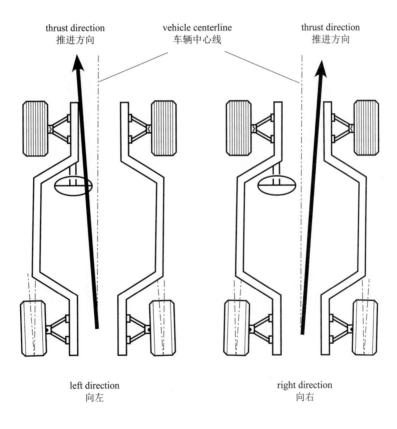

Fig.2-66 Thrust angle

★ Practice makes perfect（熟能生巧）

1. Match（对应）

_____	(1) alignment	A. 滑动
_____	(2) scuff	B. 倾斜
_____	(3) drag	C. 轮胎
_____	(4) slip	D. 稳定性
_____	(5) caster	E. 拖曳
_____	(6) spindle	F. 拖行
_____	(7) tilt	G. 调整
_____	(8) stability	H. 轴
_____	(9) tire	I. 外倾角
_____	(10) adjust	J. 内倾
_____	(11) axle	K. 轴踵
_____	(12) camber	L. 前束
_____	(13) inclination	M. 心轴
_____	(14) toe	N. 主销后倾角
_____	(15) toe in	O. 校正

2. Choice（选择）

_____ (1) Which of the following statements about a good wheel alignment is not true?
　　A. better fuel economy　　B. shorter tire life
　　C. easier steering　　D. increased safety

_____ (2) Which of these is the first angle adjusted during a wheel alignment?
　　A. SAI　　B. camber
　　C. toe in　　D. caster

_____ (3) The purpose of checking camber is to make sure that the tire is:
　　A. vertical to the road　　B. parallel to the road
　　C. vertical to the steering pivots　　D. none of the above

_____ (4) Which of these can help the vehicle's steering system return to straight ahead after a turn?

    A. SAI   B. camber   C. toe in   D. caster

_____ (5) The sum of the camber angle and the SAI angle is called the:

    A. SAI angle   B. camber

    C. toe in   D. included angle

_____ (6) Which of the following statements is wrong?

    A. toe is critical as a tire-wearing angle

    B. incorrect toe adjustment will not cause the tires to wear

    C. backward tilt is called positive caster

    D. none of the above

3. Translation（翻译）

(1) Wheel alignment is a check of how the wheels contact the pavement.

_____

(2) Caster is designed to provide steering stability.

_____

(3) The purpose of checking camber is to make sure the tire is vertical to the road.

_____

(4) The SAI helps the vehicles steering system return to straight ahead after a turn.

_____

(5) Actually, toe is critical as a tire-wearing angle.

_____

(6) If rear toe does not parallel the vehicle centerline, a thrust direction to the left or right is created.

_____

3 Tire and wheel（轮胎与车轮）

Vocabulary

primary ['praiməri]	adj.	主要的
traction ['trækʃən]	n.	牵引力
absorb [əb'sɔ:b]	v.	吸收
shock [ʃɔk]	n.	震动
carry ['kæri]	v.	运送
withstand [wið'stænd]	v.	抵抗
torque [tɔ:k]	n.	转矩
metric ['metrik]	adj.	公制的
size [saiz]	v.	按一定尺寸制作
according to [ə'kɔ:diŋ tu]		根据
application [ˌæpli'keiʃn]	n.	应用
physical ['fizikl]	adj.	物理的
mold [məuld]	v.	铸造

1) Metric tire sizes

Tires are sized according to the application in which they are to be used and their physical size. The size of the tire must be molded into the side of that tire. Most tires today are sized according to metric standards. Shown in Fig.2-67.

2) Functions of tire

The primary purpose of tires is to provide traction. Tires also help the suspension absorb road shocks. They are also designed to carry the weight of the vehicle, withstand side thrust over varying speeds, and transfer braking and driving torque to the road. The tire structure is shown in Fig.2-68.

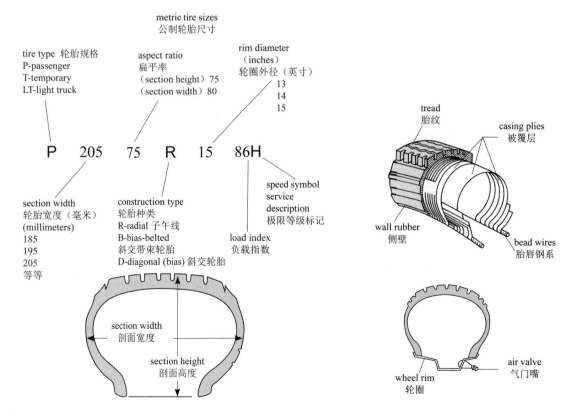

Fig.2-67 Metric tire sizes

Fig.2-68 Structures of tire

3) Inflation pressure

A properly inflated tire gives the best tire life, riding comfort, handling stability and gas mileage for normal driving conditions. Too little air pressure can result in tire squeal and hard steering. Too high air pressure can cause a hard ride and rapid wear at the center of the tire. Shown in Fig.2-69.

4) Wheel

Tires are mounted on rims made of steel, aluminum, or other strong materials. The parts of the wheel are shown in Fig.2-70. The 14-inch wheel is used for most cars. Most manufacturers recommend that a wheel be replaced if it is bent or leaks air.

Vocabulary

inflate [in'fleit]	v. 充气
comfort ['kʌmfət]	n. 舒适
handle ['hændl]	v. 操纵
mileage ['mailidʒ]	n. 英里数
squeal [skwi:l]	n. 发出长而尖的声音
rapid ['ræpid]	adj. 迅速的
mount [maunt]	v. 安装
rim [rim]	n. 轮圈
aluminum [ə'lju:minəm]	n. 铝
manufacturer [ˌmænju'fæktʃərə(r)]	n. 制造商
recommend [ˌrekə'mend]	v. 建议
replace [ri'pleis]	v. 更换
bent [bent]	v. 弯曲
leak [li:k]	v. 泄漏

under inflation
充气不足
tread contact with road
胎纹与路面接触部分

proper inflation
适当充气
tread contact with road
胎纹与路面接触部分

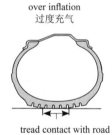
over inflation
过度充气
tread contact with road
胎纹与路面接触部分

shoulders of tread worn
胎纹两肩磨损

center of tread worn
中心磨损

Fig.2-69　Inflation pressure

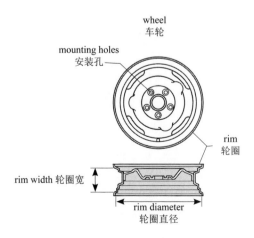

Fig.2-70　Wheel

Vocabulary

ridge [ridʒ]	n. 隆起
event [i'vent]	n. 事件
blowout ['bləuaut]	n. 车胎爆裂
tend [tend]	v. 倾向于
improve [im'pru:v]	v. 增加
type [taip]	n. 类型
variety [və'raiəti]	n. 种类
cast [ka:st]	n. 铸造
wire ['waiə(r)]	n. 金属线
consumer [kən'sju:mə(r)]	n. 消费者
purchase ['pə:tʃəs]	v. 购买
magnesium [mæg'ni:ziəm]	n. 镁

5) Safety rim

Safety rims are also being used on vehicles today. The safety rim has small ridges built into the rim. As shown in Fig.2-71. In the event of a tire blowout, these ridges tend to keep the tire from moving into the dropped center and from coming off the wheel. Thus, safety is improved.

6) Wheel types

A variety of wheels are being manufactured today. Generally, as shown in Fig.2-72, wheels are of three types: the disk wheel, the cast aluminum wheel and the wire wheel. The consumer can also purchase a mag wheel. This type of wheel uses a light magnesium metal for the rim.

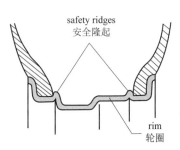

Fig.2-71　Safety rim

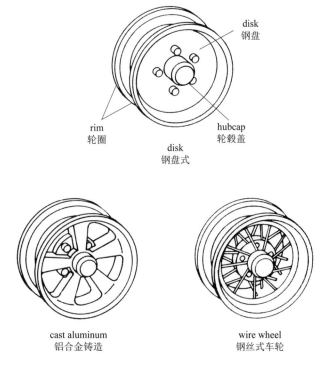

Fig.2-72　Wheel types

★ Practice makes perfect （熟能生巧）

1. Match（对应）

_____	(1) wheel	A.	铸造
_____	(2) absorb	B.	转矩
_____	(3) shock	C.	充气
_____	(4) metric	D.	轮圈
_____	(5) mold	E.	铝
_____	(6) torque	F.	弯曲
_____	(7) inflate	G.	隆起
_____	(8) mileage	H.	车轮
_____	(9) rim	I.	轮胎爆裂
_____	(10) aluminum	J.	镁
_____	(11) bent	K.	英里数
_____	(12) ridge	L.	公制的
_____	(13) blowout	M.	震动
_____	(14) magnesium	N.	吸收

2. Choice（选择）

_____ (1) Which of the following is not a function of the tire?
　　A. the tire can absorb road shocks
　　B. the tire can carry the weight of the vehicle
　　C. the tire can start a car
　　D. the tire can stop a car

_____ (2) Tires are sized according to:
　　A. the application in which they are to be used
　　B. their physical size
　　C. both of the above
　　D. none of the above

_____ (3) A properly inflated tire gives the best:
　　A. tire life　　　　　　　　B. riding comfort
　　C. handling stability　　　　D. all of the above

_____ (4) Which of the following statements is not true?
   A. tires are mounted on rims
   B. the 20-inch wheel is used for most cars
   C. the safety rim has small ridges built into the rim
   D. when a wheel is bent, it must be replaced

_____ (5) Technician A says that most tires are sized according to metric standards. Technician B says the primary purpose of tires is to provide traction. Who is right?
   A. A only   B. B only
   C. both A and B   D. neither A nor B

_____ (6) When tires are not properly inflated, too little air pressure can result in:
   A. tire squeal   B. easy steering
   C. a hard ride   D. rapid wear at the center of the tires

3. Translation（翻译）

(1) The primary purpose of tires is to provide traction.

(2) Tires are sized according to the application in which they are to be used and their physical size.

(3) A properly inflated tire gives the best tire life and riding comfort.

(4) Most manufacturers recommend that a wheel be replaced if it is bent or leaks air.

(5) Generally, wheels are of three types: the disk wheel, the cast aluminum wheel and the wire wheel.

4 Suspension system（悬架系统）

1) Components of suspension system

The suspension system on an automobile includes such components as the springs, shock absorbers, struts, torsion bars, axles and connecting linkages. These components are designed to support the body and frame, the engine and the drivelines. Without these systems, the comfort and ease of driving the vehicle would be reduced. The system is shown is Fig.2-73.

2) Types of suspension systems

The suspension systems are of two basic types: the solid axle suspension system and the independent suspension system, shown in Fig.2-74. In solid axle systems, a wheel is mounted at each end of a solid, or undivided axle. On the contrary, independent suspension systems provide a separate mounting for each wheel.

Vocabulary

shock absorber [ʃɔk əb'sɔ:bə]	n. 减振器
strut [strʌt]	n. 支柱
torsion bar ['tɔ:ʃən bɑ:]	n. 扭力杆
frame [freim]	n. 车架
driveline [draivlain]	n. 动力传输线
solid ['sɔlid]	adj. 非独立悬架
independent [ˌindi'pendənt]	adj. 独立的
undivided [ˌʌndi'vaidid]	adj. 不分离的
contrary [kən'treəri]	n. 相反
separate ['seprət]	adj. 分离的

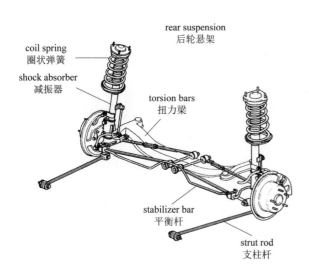

Fig.2-73 Components of suspension system

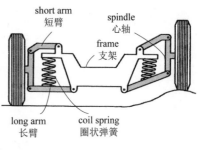

Fig.2-74 Types of suspension systems

Vocabulary

core [kɔː(r)]	n. 核心
nearly ['niəli]	adj. 几乎
coil [kɔil]	n. 线圈
leaf [liːf]	n. 叶片
original [ə'ridʒənl]	adj. 最初的
damp [dæmp]	v. 抑制振动；减振
motion ['məuʃən]	n. 运动
device [di'vais]	n. 装置
condition [kən'diʃn]	n. 状况

3) Springs

Spring are the core of almost all suspension systems. Various types of springs as shown in Fig.2-75. are used in suspension systems: coil, torsion bar, leaf and air springs. The purpose of the springs is to absorb road shock and return to their original position.

4) Shock absorbers

Shock absorbers damp or control motion in a vehicle. The shock absorber, as shown in Fig.2-76, is placed parallel to the upward and downward motion of the car. Today's conventional shock absorber is a velocity-sensitive hydraulic damping device. The faster it moves the more resistance it has. This allows it to automatically adjust to road conditions.

Fig.2-75　Springs

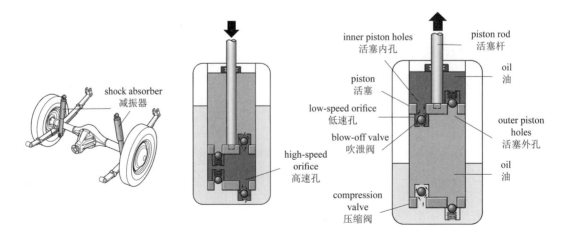

Fig.2-76　Shock absorbers

★ Practice makes perfect（熟能生巧）

1. Match（对应）

_____ (1) shock absorber   A. 车架
_____ (2) strut   B. 减振器
_____ (3) torsion bar   C. 非独立悬架
_____ (4) frame   D. 动力传输线
_____ (5) solid   E. 线圈
_____ (6) undivided   F. 装置
_____ (7) driveline   G. 状况
_____ (8) separate   H. 支柱
_____ (9) core   I. 抑制振动；减振
_____ (10) damp   J. 叶片
_____ (11) motion   K. 运动
_____ (12) coil   L. 核心
_____ (13) leaf   M. 分离的
_____ (14) device   N. 不分离的
_____ (15) condition   O. 扭力杆

2. Choice（选择）

_____ (1) Which of the following is not a part of the suspension system?
　　A. spring   B. shock absorber
　　C. torsion bar   D. wheels

_____ (2) The suspension system is designed to support:
　　A. the body   B. the engine
　　C. the drivlines   D. all of the above

_____ (3) Which of the following statements is not true?

A. independent suspension systems provide a separate mounting for each wheel

B. without the suspension system, the ease of driving the vehicle would be increased

C. the spring is the core of nearly all suspension systems

D. shock absorbers can damp motion in a vehicle

_____ (4) In solid axle suspension systems, a wheel is mounted at each end of a:

A. undivided axle

B. divided axle

C. separated axle

D. none of the above

3. Translation（翻译）

(1) Without the suspension system, the comfort and ease of driving the vehicle would be reduced.

_____

(2) Independent suspension systems provide a separate mounting for each wheel.

_____

(3) The purpose of the springs is to absorb road shock and then return to their original position.

_____

(4) Shock absorbers damp or control motion in a vehicle.

_____

5 Brake system (制动系统)

1) Brakes

Brakes, which are located at each wheel, utilize friction to slow and stop the automobile. The brake pedal is connected to a plunger in a master cylinder, which is filled with hydraulic fluid. When the brake pedal is depressed, the force is increased by the master cylinder and transferred through brake hoses and lines to the four brake assemblies. As shown in Fig.2-77.

2) Types of brake systems

Two types of brakes are used on automobiles: disc brakes and drum brakes. Shown in Fig.2-78. Many automobiles use a combination of the two types: disc brakes at the front wheels and drum brakes at the rear wheels. Nowadays most vehicles have power-assisted brakes.

Vocabulary

utilize ['ju:təlaiz]	v. 使用
pedal ['pedl]	n. 踏板
plunger ['plʌndʒə(r)]	n. 柱塞
master cylinder ['mɑ:stə(r) 'silində(r)]	n. 总泵
depress [di'pres]	v. 压下
assembly [ə'sembli]	n. 总成
disc [disk]	n. 制动盘
drum [drʌm]	n. 制动鼓
combination [ˌkɔmbi'neiʃn]	n. 结合
nowadays ['nauədeiz]	adv. 当今
power-assisted [pauə ə'sistid]	adj. 动力辅助的

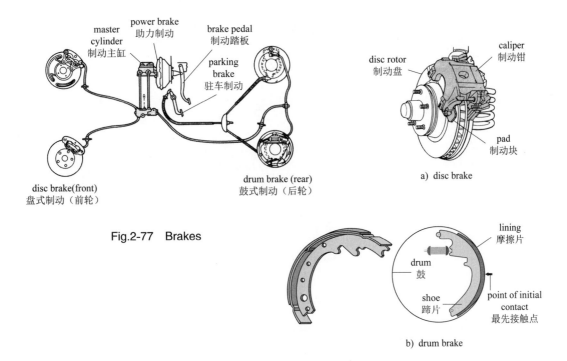

Fig.2-77 Brakes

Fig.2-78 Types of brake systems

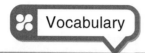

passenger ['pæsindʒə(r)] n. 乘客
extra ['ekstrə] adj. 额外的
booster ['bu:stə(r)] n. 增压器
multiply v. 使（成倍地）增加
['mʌltiplai]

3) Power brakes

Power brakes are used on many passenger cars today. Power brakes are designed to have an extra pressure by an equipment called booster. When the brake pedal is applied, the booster unit multiplies the pedal force for the master cylinder. This means the operator puts less force on the brake pedal, making it easier to stop the car. Shown in Fig.2-79.

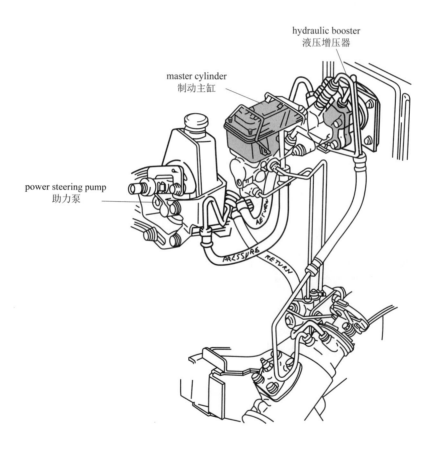

Fig.2-79　Power brakes

4) Anti-lock brake system (ABS)

In a conventional brake system, if the brake pedal is depressed excessively, the wheel can lock up before the vehicle comes to stop. Anti-lock braking systems are designed to prevent wheel lockup under heavy braking conditions, and help the driver retain directional stability, stop sooner and retain maximum control of the vehicle. As shown in Fig.2-80.

5) Drum parking brakes

The parking brake keeps a vehicle from rolling while it is parked. Shown in Fig.2-81. It is important to remember that the parking brake is not a part of the vehicle's hydraulic braking system. It works mechanically, using a lever assembly connected through a cable system to the rear drum service brake. Parking brakes can be either hand or foot operated.

Vocabulary

anti-lock ['æntilɔk]		n. 防锁死
lock [lɔk]		v. 锁
lockup ['lɔkʌp]		n. 锁死
retain [ri'tein]		v. 保持
directional [də'rekʃənl]		adj. 方向的
park [pɑ:k]		v. 停车
roll [rəul]		v. 滚动
mechanically [mi'kænikəli]		adv. 机械式地
lever ['li:və(r)]		n. 杠杆
cable ['keibl]		n. 钢索

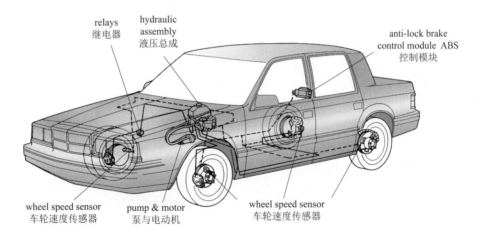

Fig.2-80 ABS

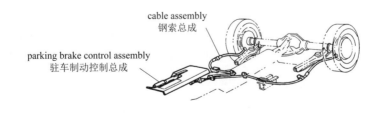

Fig.2-81 Drum parking brakes

★ **Practice makes perfect**（熟能生巧）

1. Match（对应）

_____ (1) pedal   A. 柱塞

_____ (2) disc   B. 主缸

_____ (3) drum   C. 动力辅助

_____ (4) plunger   D. 增压器

_____ (5) master cylinder E. 踏板

_____ (6) assembly   F. 制动鼓

_____ (7) power-assisted   G. 制动盘

_____ (8) booster   H. 总成

_____ (9) anti-lock   I. 防锁死

_____ (10) lockup   J. 停车

_____ (11) roll   K. 杠杆

_____ (12) park   L. 钢索

_____ (13) lever   M. 压下

_____ (14) cable   N. 滚动

_____ (15) depress   O. 锁死

2. Choice（选择）

_____ (1) Which of the following systems can slow and stop the automobile?

   A. the brake system   B. the suspension system

   C. the cooling system   D. the steering system

_____ (2) When the brake pedal is depressed, the force is increased by:

   A. the slave cylinder   B. the master cylinder

   C. the brake hoses   D. the brake lines

_____ (3) Power brakes are designed to have an extra pressure by an equipment called a:

   A. pump   B. absorber

   C. booster   D. cylinder

_____ (4) Which of the following statements about the antilock braking sytem is not true?
    A. it can prevent wheel lockup
    B. it can help the driver to retain directional stability
    C. it can't stop the vehicle faster
    D. it can retain maximum control of the vehicle

_____ (5) Which of these can keep a vehicle from rolling while it is parked?
    A. the parking brake
    B. the shock absorber
    C. the ABS
    D. none of the above

3. Translation（翻译）

(1) Brakes, which are located at each wheel, utilize friction to slow and stop the automobile.

_____

(2) Two types of brakes are used on automobiles: disc brakes and drum brakes.

_____

(3) Power brakes are designed to have an extra pressure by an equipment called a booster.

_____

(4) Anti-lock braking system is designed to prevent wheel lockup under heavy braking conditions.

_____

(5) The parking brake keeps a vehicle from rolling while it is parked.

_____

2.2.3 Electrical systems（电气系统）

1 Battery（蓄电池）

Vocabulary

battery ['bætəri]	n.	蓄电池
receive [ri'si:v]	v.	接受
sufficient [sə'fiʃənt]	adj.	足够的
crank [kræŋk]	v.	发动；摇转
starter ['stɑ:tə(r)]	n.	起动机
ignition [ig'niʃn]	n.	点火
solenoid ['səulinɔid]	n.	电磁阀
construction [kən'strʌkʃn]	n.	结构
grid [grid]	n.	格状物
positive ['pɔzətiv]	adj.	正的
plate [pleit]	n.	极板
negative ['negətiv]	adj.	负的
element ['elimənt]	n.	分电池
electrolyte [i'lektrəulait]	n.	电解液

1) Purpose of the battery

The battery receives, stores and makes electrical energy available to the automobile. The purpose of the battery is to provide sufficient electrical energy to crank the starter and operate the ignition system, computers, solenoid, lights and other electrical components. See Fig.2-82.

2) Battery construction

The storage battery consists of grids, positive plates, negative plates, separators, elements, a container, cell covers, electrolyte and vent caps. See Fig.2-83.

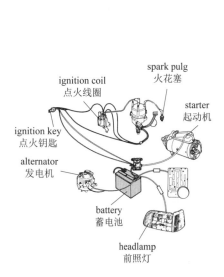

Fig.2-82 Functions of battery

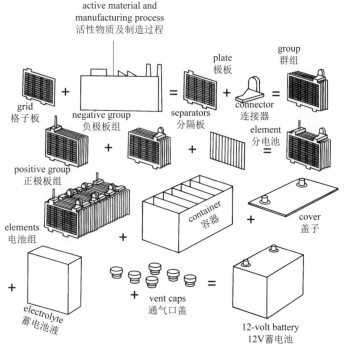

Fig.2-83 Battery construction

3) Electrolyte

The electrolyte in a battery is a combination of water and sulfuric acid. Normally, the ratio of acid to water is 40% acid to 60% distilled water. The specific gravity of water (1.000) mixed with acid (1.835) is equal to an electrolyte solution of 1.270. Shown in Fig.2-84. Electrolyte is very corrosive. If electrolyte gets on you, immediately wash yourself with baking soda and water.

4) Battery charging

Both fast and slow-charging units are used to recharge batteries. Each has its advantages. Fast charges can recharge most batteries in about 1 hour. However, batteries must be in good condition to accept a fast charge. The slow charge is defined as charging the battery at a low ampere rating over a long period of time. Fig.2-85 shows two style of charging connections.

Vocabulary

sulfuric [sʌl'fju:rik]	adj. 硫磺的
acid ['æsid]	n. 酸
distilled [dis'tild]	adj. 蒸馏的
specific gravity [spə'sifik 'grævəti]	n. 密度
solution [sə'lju:ʃn]	n. 溶液
corrosive [kə'rəusiv]	adj. 腐蚀性的
baking soda ['beikiŋ 'səudə]	n. 碳酸氢钠
charge [tʃɑ:dʒ]	v. 充电
advantage [əd'vɑ:ntidʒ]	n. 优点
accept [ək'sept]	v. 接受

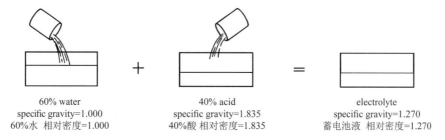

Fig.2-84 Electrolyte

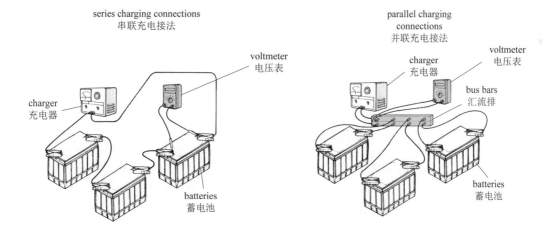

Fig.2-85 Battery charging

★ Practice makes perfect （熟能生巧）

1. Match （对应）

_____	(1) battery	A. 起动机
_____	(2) crank	B. 电磁阀
_____	(3) starter	C. 硫磺的
_____	(4) ignition	D. 格状物
_____	(5) solenoid	E. 蒸馏的
_____	(6) sulfuric	F. 电解液
_____	(7) acid	G. 发动
_____	(8) grid	H. 蓄电池
_____	(9) plate	I. 点火
_____	(10) distilled	J. 酸性的
_____	(11) specific gravity	K. 腐蚀性的
_____	(12) electrolyte	L. 溶液
_____	(13) corrosive	M. 碳酸氢钠
_____	(14) baking soda	N. 密度
_____	(15) solution	O. 极板

2. Choice （选择）

_____ (1) Which of the following statements about the battery is true?
　　A. the battery can't receive electrical energy
　　B. the battery can't store electrical energy
　　C. the battery can't provide the power for lighting systema
　　D. the battery can provide electrical energy to crank the starter

_____ (2) Which of these is not a part of the battery?
　　A. positive plate　　B. negative plate
　　C. electrolyte　　D. disc

_____ (3) The electrolyte in a battery is a combination of water and:
        A. sulfuric acid   B. air
        C. gasoline   D. diesel

_____ (4) If electrolyte gets on you, immediately wash yourself with:
        A. milk   B. water
        C. sulfuric acid   D. wine

_____ (5) Fast charges can recharge most batteries in about:
        A. 5 hours   B. 3 hours
        C. 1 hour   D. 10 minutes

3. Translation（翻译）

(1) The battery receives, stores and makes electrical energy available to the automobile.

_____

(2) The electrolyte in a battery is a combination of water and sulfuric acid.

_____

(3) If electrolyte gets on you, immediately wash yourself with baking soda and water.

_____

(4) Batteries must be in good condition to accept a fast charge.

_____

2 Ignition system(点火系统)

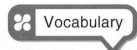

main [mein]	adj. 主要的
generate ['dʒenəreit]	v. 产生
spark [spɑ:k]	n. 火花
maintain [mein'tein]	v. 维持
deliver [di'livə(r)]	v. 传递

1) Purpose of the ignition system

For each cylinder in an engine, the ignition system has three main jobs. First, it must generate an electrical spark to ignite the air-fuel mixture. Secondly, it must maintain the spark long enough to allow for the combustion. Lastly, it must deliver the spark to each cylinder that combustion can begin at the right time. See Fig.2-86.

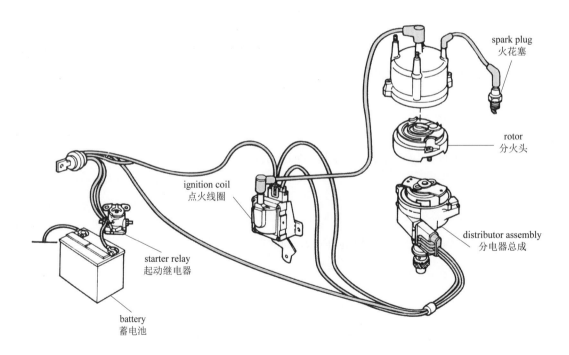

Fig.2-86 Ignition system

2) Primary and secondary circuits

All ignition systems consist of two interconnected electrical circuits: a primary circuit and a secondary circuit. The primary circuit includes the battery, the ignition switch, the resistance wire, the ignition coil and the distributor points. The secondary circuit carries high voltage to the spark plugs. It includes the ignition coil (secondary coil winding), the distributor rotor and the spark plug. Shown in Fig.2-87.

3) Distributor

Contact point and many electronic ignition systems include an ignition distributor. It is a separate unit that triggers the ignition coil to produce a series of high-voltage surges. Distributes the high-voltage surges from the ignition coil to the spark plugs. The spark advance mechanism changes spark timing. See Fig.2-88.

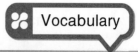

Vocabulary

secondary ['sekəndəri]	adj. 二次的
interconnected [ˌintəkə'nektid]	adj. 相连的
switch [switʃ]	n. 开关
distributor [di'stribjətə(r)]	n. 分电器
point [pɔint]	n. 接点
voltage ['vəultidʒ]	n. 电压
winding ['waindiŋ]	n. 绕线
rotor ['rəutə(r)]	n. 分火头
contact point ['kɔntækt pɔint]	n. 白金接点
trigger ['trigə(r)]	v. 触发
mechanism ['mekənizəm]	n. 机械装置
timing ['taimiŋ]	n. 正时

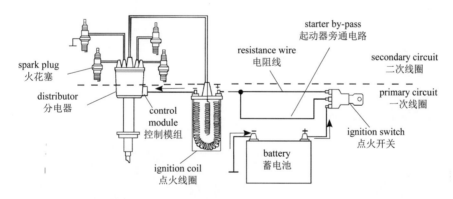

Fig.2-87 Primary and secondary

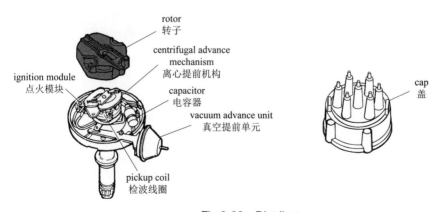

Fig.2-88 Distributor

Vocabulary

ceramic [sə'ræmik]	adj.	陶瓷的
insulator ['insjuleitə(r)]	n.	绝缘体
shell [ʃel]	n.	外壳
current ['kʌrənt]	n.	电流
arc [ɑ:k]	n.	电弧
offer ['ɔfə(r)]	v.	提供
network ['netwə:k]	n.	网路
central ['sentrəl]	adj.	中央的
microprocessor [ˌmaikrəu'prəusesə(r)]	n.	微处理器
regard [ri'gɑ:d]	v.	视……而定
module ['mɔdju:l]	n.	模块
program ['prəugræm]	n.	程序
memory ['meməri]	n.	存储器

4) Spark plug

The spark plug uses a high voltage (10 000V to 30 000V) to ignite the air-fuel mixture. The three main parts of a spark plug are the steel core, the ceramic core, or insulator; and a pair of electrodes, one insulated in the core and the other grounded on the shell. Current flows through the center of the plug and causes arc from the tip of the center electrode to the ground electrode. See Fig.2-89.

5) Computer-controlled electronic ignition

Computer-controlled ignition systems offer continuous spark timing control through a network of engine sensors and a central microprocessor. As shown in Fig.2-90. Based on the inputs it receives, the central microprocessor or computer makes decisions regarding spark timing and sends signals to the ignition module to fire the spark plugs according to the inputs and the programs in its memory.

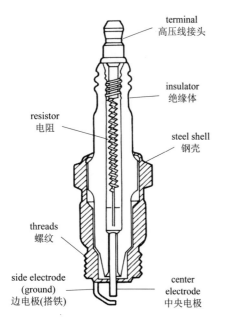

Fig.2-89 Components of a typical spark plug

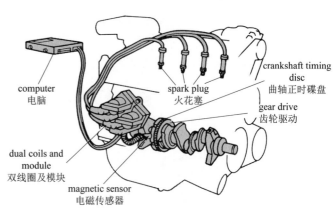

Fig.2-90 Computer-controlled electronic ignition

★ Practice makes perfect（熟能生巧）

1. Match（对应）

_____ (1) generate　　　　　A. 白金接点

_____ (2) spark　　　　　　B. 分电器

_____ (3) secondary　　　　C. 绕线

_____ (4) contact point　　D. 正时

_____ (5) trigger　　　　　E. 绝缘体

_____ (6) switch　　　　　F. 电压

_____ (7) distributor　　　G. 二次的

_____ (8) voltage　　　　　H. 电流

_____ (9) winding　　　　　I. 模块

_____ (10) timing　　　　　J. 微处理器

_____ (11) insulator　　　　K. 网络

_____ (12) current　　　　　L. 开关

_____ (13) network　　　　　M. 触发

_____ (14) microprocessor　N. 火花

_____ (15) module　　　　　O. 产生

2. Choice（选择）

_____ (1) Which of the following statements about the ignition system is wrong?

　　A. it must generate an electrical spark

　　B. it must maintain that spark long enough

　　C. it must deliver the spark to each cylinder

　　D. it can provide electrical energy to crank the starter

_____ (2) Which of these is not the component of the primary circuit?

　　A. the spark plug　　　　B. the battery

　　C. the distributor points　D. the ignition switch

_____ (3) Technician A says that many electronic ignition systems include an ignition distributor. Technician B says that the spark advance mechanism can change spark timing. Who is right?

    A. A only   B. B only

    C. both A and B   D. neither A nor B

_____ (4) Which of the following statements about the spark plug is right?

    A. it uses a low voltage to ignite the air-fuel mixture

    B. it uses a high voltage to ignite the air-fuel mixture

    C. it contains 4 electrodes

    D. all the electrodes are grounded

_____ (5) Which of these can make decisions and send signals to the ignition module to fire the spark plug?

    A. the distributor   B. the primary circuit

    C. the central microprocessor   D. the ignition coil

3. Translation（翻译）

(1) The ignition system can generate an electrical spark to ignite the air-fuel mixture.

_____

(2) The secondary circuit carries high voltage to the spark plugs.

_____

(3) Contact point and many electronic ignition systems include an ignition distributor.

_____

(4) The spark plug uses a high voltage to ignite the air-fuel mixture.

_____

(5) Based on the inputs it receives, the central microprocessor makes decisions and sends signals to the ignition module to fire the spark plugs.

3 Starting system（起动系统）

1) Components and functions

The only function of the starting system is to crank the engine fast enough to run. A typical starting system has six basic components. They are the battery, ignition switch, battery cables, magnetic switch, starter motor and the starter safety switch. A considerable amount of mechanical power is necessary to start a car engine. About 2 horsepower, or 250 to 500 amps of electricity, is normally needed. The starting system is shown in Fig.2-91.

2) The starter motor

Basically, the starter motor consists of a housing, field coils, an armature, a commutator and brushes and end frames. The main difference between designs is in the drive mechanism used to engage the flywheel. The starter is a powerful motor that can crank the engine fast enough to start the car. But the starter can only operate for short periods of time without rest. The starter motor is shown in Fig.2-92.

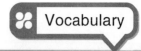

Vocabulary

typical ['tipikl]	adj. 典型的
magnetic [mæg'netik]	adj. 磁性的
considerable [kən'sidərəbl]	adj. 相当大的
horsepower ['hɔːspauə(r)]	n. 马力
field ['fiːld]	n. 磁场
armature ['ɑːmətʃə(r)]	n. 电枢
commutator ['kɔmjuteitə]	n. 整流器
brush [brʌʃ]	n. 电刷
engage [in'geidʒ]	v. 啮合
period ['piəriəd]	n. 周期

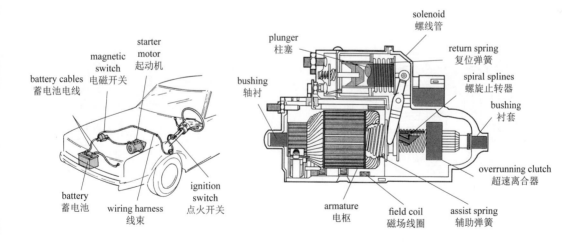

Fig.2-91 Starting system　　　　Fig.2-92 Starter motor

Vocabulary

overrunning [ˌəuvəˈrʌniŋ]	adj.	超速的
clutch [klʌtʃ]	n.	离合器
through [θruː]	prep.	经过
spin [spin]	v.	旋转
disengage [ˌdisinˈgeidʒ]	v.	脱离
release [riˈliːs]	v.	释放
reduction [riˈdʌkʃən]	n.	减少
between [biˈtwiːn]	prep.	在……之间
ring gear [riŋ giə(r)]	n.	齿圈

3) Overrunning clutch

When the engine starts and runs, if the starter motor is still connected to the engine through the flywheel, it will spin at a very high speed. To prevent this, an overrunning clutch is used to disengage the starter. When the flywheel spins the pinion faster than the armature, the overrunning clutch releases the rollers, unlocking the pinion gear from the armature shaft. See Fig.2-93.

4) Gear reduction systems

On certain vehicles, a gear reduction system is used between the starter and the pinion gear. Its purpose is to increase the amount of torque during starting of the engine. The gears are designed to reduce the speed of the pinion gear (keeping the starter at the same speed), thus producing more torque at the flywheel ring gear. Fig.2-94 shows a system using a single reduction gear.

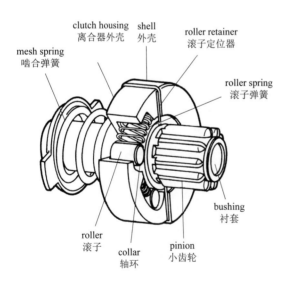

Fig.2-93 Overrunning clutch

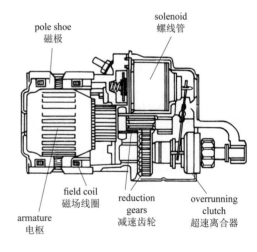

Fig.2-94 Gear reduction system

★ Practice makes perfect （熟能生巧）

1. Match （对应）

_____ (1) magnetic   A. 整流器
_____ (2) horsepower   B. 电刷
_____ (3) field   C. 接合
_____ (4) armature   D. 周期
_____ (5) commutator   E. 释放
_____ (6) brush   F. 齿圈
_____ (7) engage   G. 马力
_____ (8) period   H. 磁性的
_____ (9) overrunning   I. 磁场
_____ (10) clutch   J. 电枢
_____ (11) spin   K. 减少
_____ (12) disengage   L. 脱离
_____ (13) reduction   M. 旋转
_____ (14) ring gear   N. 离合器
_____ (15) release   O. 超速的

2. Choice （选择）

_____ (1) The only function of the starting system is to:
　　　　　　　A. crank the engine   B. stop the engine
　　　　　　　C. cool the engine   D. lubricate the engine

_____ (2) Technician A says that the starter can only operate for short periods of time without rest. Technician B says that about 2 horsepower is normally needed to start a car engine. Who is right?
　　　　　　　A. A only   B. B only
　　　　　　　C. both A and B   D. neither A nor B

_____ (3) Which of these is used to disengage the starter?

    A. overrunning clutch

    B. gear reduction system

    C. flywheel

    D. switch

_____ (4) Which of the following statements about the starting system is wrong?

    A. the starter is a powerful motor

    B. a typical starting system has six basic components

    C. the gear reduction system can increase the amount of torque

    D. the gear reduction system can increase the speed of the pinion gear

3. Translation（翻译）

(1) The only function of the starting system is to crank the engine fast enough to run.

_____

(2) The starter can only operate for short periods of time without rest.

_____

(3) The overrunning clutch is used to disengage the starter.

_____

(4) On certain vehicles a gear reduction system is used between the starter and the pinion gear.

_____

4 Charging system（充电系统）

1) Purpose of the charging system

The charging system is designed to recharge and maintain the battery's state of charge. It also provides electrical power for the ignition system, air conditioner, heater, lights, radio and all electrical accessories when the engine is running.

In addition to the battery, the charging system includes the alternator or generator, voltage regulator, indicator light and the necessary wiring. See Fig.2-95.

2) Alternator construction

Fig.2-96 illustrates the major parts of an alternator.

(1) The rotor: is a rotating magnetic field inside the alternator.

(2) The stator: the rotor rotates inside the stator; the stator produces alternating electric current.

(3) The regulator: provides enough current to operate the vehicle's electrical equipments, but not so much that the battery is overcharged.

Vocabulary

heater ['hi:tə]   n. 加热器；暖气机
radio ['reidiəu]   n. 收音机
accessory [ək'sesəri]   n. 配件
alternator   n. 交流发电机
['ɔ:ltəneitə(r)]
generator   n. 直流发电机
['dʒenəreitə(r)]
indicator ['indikeitə(r)]   n. 指示器
wiring ['waiəriŋ]   n. 配线
illustrate ['iləstreit]   v. 图解
inside ['in'said]   adj. 在…之内
stator ['steitə]   n. 定子
equipment [i'kwipmənt]   n. 设备
overcharge   v. 过量充电
[,əuvə'tʃɑ:dʒ]

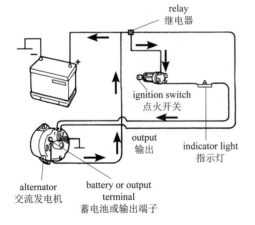

Fig.2-95 Charging system

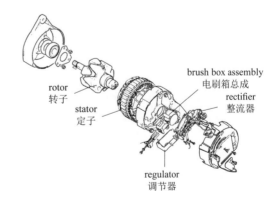

Fig.2-96 Alternator construction

Vocabulary

pole [pəul]   n. 极
belt [belt]   n. 皮带
stationary ['steiʃənri]   adj. 固定的
induce [in'dju:s]   v. 感应
amperage ['æmpəridʒ]   n. 安培数
arrange [ə'reindʒ]   v. 安排
waveform ['weivfɔ:m]   n. 波形

3) The rotor

As shown in Fig.2-97, the rotor assembly consists of a drive shaft, coil and two pole pieces. A pulley mounted on one end of the shaft allows the rotor to be belt driven by the crankshaft pulley. The rotor is a rotating magnetic field inside the alternator. Magnetic field lines around the rotor cut the stator windings and produce an inductive voltage in the stator windings.

4) The stator

The stator is the stationary member of the alternator. It is made up of a number of wires, into which the voltage is induced by the rotating magnetic field. Most alternators use three windings to generate the required amperage output. The windings are arranged so that a separate AC voltage waveform is induced in each windings. See Fig.2-98.

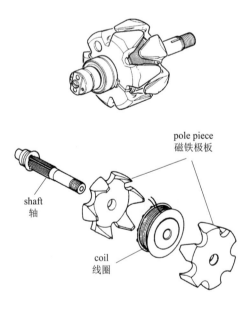

Fig.2-97 Rotor

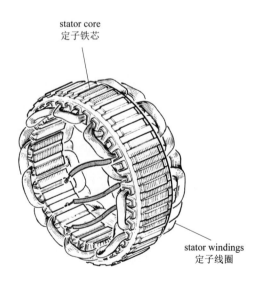

Fig.2-98 Stator

5) Voltage regulator

The output of the alternator must be regulated and controlled. If the voltage is too high, the light bulbs may burn out and the battery may overheat. Fig.2-99a) shows a three-unit regulator. It has a cutout relay, a voltage regulator, and a current regulator to control the output. Fig.2-99 shows the theory of regulator.

Vocabulary

regulate ['regjuleit]	v. 调整
control [kən'trəul]	v. 控制
bulb [bʌlb]	n. 电灯泡
overheat [,əuvə'hi:t]	v. 过热
cutout ['kʌtaut]	n. 切断
relay ['ri:lei]	n. 继电器

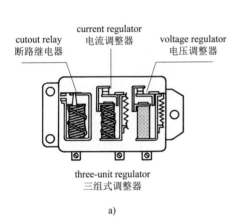
a)

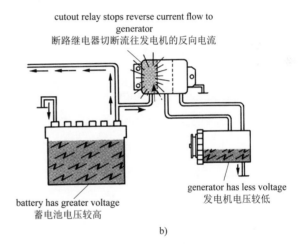
b)

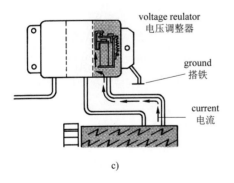
c)

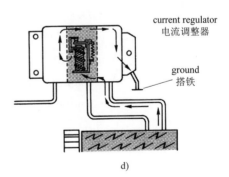
d)

Fig.2-99　Regulator

★ Practice makes perfect（熟能生巧）

1. Match（对应）

_____ (1) accessory   A. 定子

_____ (2) alternator   B. 配线

_____ (3) stator   C. 配件

_____ (4) overcharge   D. 皮带

_____ (5) generator   E. 电灯泡

_____ (6) indicator   F. 感应

_____ (7) wiring   G. 继电器

_____ (8) pole   H. 调整

_____ (9) belt   I. 波形

_____ (10) induce   J. 安培数

_____ (11) amperage   K. 指示器

_____ (12) waveform   L. 交流发电机

_____ (13) bulb   M. 直流发电机

_____ (14) regulate   N. 极

_____ (15) relay   O. 过量充电

2. Choice（选择）

_____ (1) Which of the following statements about the charging system is wrong?
- A. it can provide power for the ignition system when the engine is not running
- B. it is designed to recharge the battery
- C. it includes the alternator or generator
- D. it can provide electrical power for the air conditioner

_____ (2) Which of the following statements about the alternator is right?
- A. the stator is a rotating magnetic field
- B. the rotor rotates inside the stator
- C. the rotor can produce alternating electric current
- D. the regulator can not protect the battery

_____ (3) What will happen when the magnetic field lines around the rotor
　　　　　　　　　 Cut the stator windings?
　　　　　　　　　 A. nothing
　　　　　　　　　 B. the rotor will hurt the stator windings
　　　　　　　　　 C. a voltage is produced in the stator windings
　　　　　　　　　 D. the stator windings will move to one side

_____ (4) Which of the following parts is not included in the voltage regulator?
　　　　　　　　　 A. cutout relay　　　　　　B. voltage regulator
　　　　　　　　　 C. current regulator　　　　D. brush

_____ (5) How many windings are used in most alternators?
　　　　　　　　　 A. 3　　　　B. 4　　　　C. 5　　　　D. 6

3. Translation（翻译）

(1) The charging system is designed to recharge and maintain the battery's state of charge.

_____

(2) The rotor is a rotating magnetic field inside the alternator.

_____

(3) The rotor assembly consists of a drive shaft, coil and two pole pieces.

_____

(4) Most alternators use three windings to generate the required amperage output.

_____

(5) The output of the alternator must be regulated and controlled.

_____

5 Computer system（电脑系统）

Vocabulary

information [ˌinfə'meiʃən]	n. 信息
calculation [ˌkælkju'leiʃn]	n. 计算
decision [di'siʒn]	n. 决定
service ['sə:vis]	n. 服务
manual ['mænjuəl]	n. 手册
identify [ai'dentifai]	v. 认明
include [in'klu:d]	v. 包含

1) Computer locations and names

The automotive computer is able to receive information from vehicle sensors and other components. The microprocessor inside the computer does the calculations and makes decisions of exactly what to control.

Fig.2-100 shows a view of a vehicle with many of the computers used today. There are many names used in the service manuals to identify computers. Some of the more common ones include:

ECU-Electronic Control Unit
ECM-Engine Control Module
ECM-Electronic Control Module
ECA-Electronic Control Assembly
ECCS-Electronic Computer Control System
ECECS-Electronic Constant Engine Control System
BCM-Body Control Module
PCM-Power Control Module

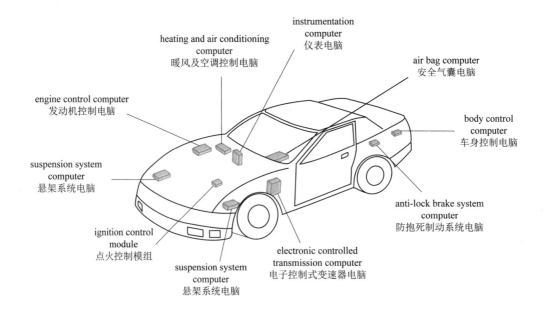

Fig.2-100 Computer locations and names

2) Computer inputs and outputs

Computers are much like the brain of human. Various inputs from an automobile are sent to the computer. Then, based upon these inputs, the computer makes a decision and controls some types of output. Fig.2-101 shows a simple example. Based upon the three inputs, the computer then makes a decision about how much fuel to put through the fuel injector.

Vocabulary

input ['input]	n. 输入
output ['autput]	n. 输出
brain [brein]	n. 脑
human ['hju:mən]	adj. 人类的
example [ig'zɑ:mpl]	n. 实例

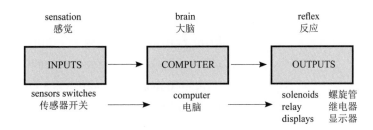

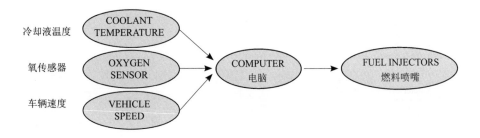

Fig.2-101 Types of input and output devices

Vocabulary

potentiometer [pə,tenʃi'ɔmitə]　n. 电位计
relationship [ri'leiʃənʃip]　n. 关系
thermistor [θə:'mistə]　n. 热敏电阻
pickup ['pikʌp]　n. 检出器
position [pə'ziʃən]　n. 位置
servomotor ['sə:vəu'məutə]　n. 伺服电动机
display [di'splei]　v. 显示
activate ['æktiveit]　v. 启动
transistor [træn'zistə(r)]　n. 晶体管
energize ['enədʒaiz]　v. 供给能量

3) Types of input and output devices

Types of input devices:

(1) Potentiometer: it can change voltage in relationship to mechanical motion.

(2) Thermistor: it changes its electrical resistance on the basic of a change in temperature.

(3) Magnetic pickup: it is used to measure the speed of a rotating object.

(4) Voltage generator: it produces a voltage based on certain inputs, such as oxygen.

(5) Switch: it simply indicates an on-off position.

Fig.2-102 shows types of output devices:

(1) Relay: it uses a small coil to control the opening and closing of another circuit.

(2) Solenoid: it uses a coil of wire to move a mechanical rod inside the coil.

(3) Servomotor: it is a motor used to turn something.

(4) Lighted display: it activates a light.

(5) Switching transistor: it is a transistor that is energized by the computer to control a greater current.

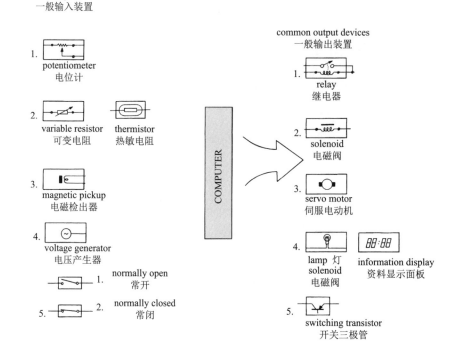

Fig.2-102　Types of input and output devices

★ Practice makes perfect（熟能生巧）

1. Match（对应）

_____ (1) information　　A. 手册

_____ (2) calculation　　B. 输入

_____ (3) decision　　C. 输出

_____ (4) service　　D. 热敏电阻

_____ (5) manual　　E. 检出器

_____ (6) input　　F. 显示

_____ (7) output　　G. 作动

_____ (8) potentiometer　　H. 伺服电动机

_____ (9) thermistor　　I. 电位计

_____ (10) pickup　　J. 计算

_____ (11) servomotor　　K. 晶体管

_____ (12) display　　L. 服务

_____ (13) activate　　M. 决定

_____ (14) transistor　　N. 供给能量

_____ (15) energize　　O. 信息

2. Choice（选择）

_____ (1) What is the function of the microprocessor?

　　A. it does the calculations

　　B. it stores the programs

　　C. it recharges the battery

　　D. all of the above

_____ (2) The computer can make decisions based upon the:

　　A. outputs　　B. inputs

　　C. printer　　D. monitor

_____ (3) Which of these can change voltage in relationship to mechanical motion?

  A. relay   B. servomotor

  C. potentiometer   D. switch

_____ (4) Which of these can control the opening and closing of Another circuit?

  A. servomotor   B. potentiometer

  C. solenoid   D. relay

_____ (5) Technician A says that the magnetic pickup is used to measure the speed of a rotating object. Technician B says that the servomotor is a motor used to turn something. Who is right?

  A. A only   B. B only   C. both A and B   D. neither A nor B

3. Translation（翻译）

(1) The microprocessor inside the computer does the calculations and makes decisions of exactly what to control.

_____

(2) Computers are much like the brain of human.

_____

(3) Various inputs from an automobile are sent to the computer.

_____

(4) The potentiometer can change voltage in relationship to mechanical motion.

_____

(5) The relay uses a small coil to control the opening and closing of another circuit.

_____

6 Body electrical system（车身电系）

1) Lighting system

The lighting system provides power to both exterior and interior lights. It consists of the headlights, parking lights, marker lights, taillights, courtesy lights, dome/map lights, instrument illumination or dash lights, headlight switch and various other control switches. Other lights that are not usually in the main lighting system are turn signal, hazard warning, back-up and stop lights. See Fig.2-103.

Vocabulary

lighting ['laitiŋ]	n. 照明
courtesy light ['kə:təsi 'lait]	n. 探照灯
instrument ['instrəmənt]	n. 仪表
illumination [i,lu:mi'neiʃn]	n. 照明
dash light	n. 仪表灯
hazard ['hæzəd]	n. 危险
panel ['pænl]	n. 镜板
array [ə'rei]	n. 阵列
speedometer [spi:'dɔmitə(r)]	n. 车速表
tachometer [tæ'kɔmitə]	n. 转速表
analog ['ænəlɔ:g]	n. 模拟
digital ['didʒitl]	adj. 数字式
data ['deitə]	n. 数据

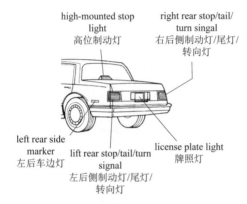

Fig.2-103 Lighting system

2) Instrument panels

As shown in Fig.2-104. Instrument panel mounts an array of electrical gauges, switches. The speedometer tells the vehicle speed and the tachometer indicates engine speed. The fuel level gauge indicates the fuel level in the fuel tank. The oil pressure gauge indicates engine oil pressure. The two basic types of instrument panel displays are analog and digital. Analog displays are useful when the driver must see something quickly and the exact reading is not important. For example, the driver does not need to know exactly how many rpm the engine is running. The most important thing is how fast the engine is reaching the red line on the gauge. A digital display is better for showing exact data such as miles or operating hours.

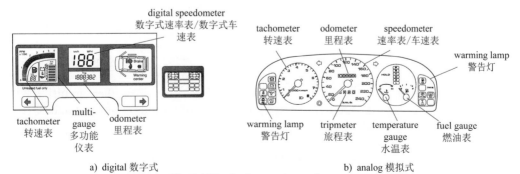

a) digital 数字式   b) analog 模拟式

Fig.2-104 Instrument panels

★ Practice makes perfect（熟能生巧）

1. Match（对应）

_____ (1) lighting   A. 室内照明灯

_____ (2) exterior   B. 仪表

_____ (3) interior   C. 车速表

_____ (4) courtesy light   D. 数字式

_____ (5) dome light   E. 模拟式

_____ (6) analog   F. 转速表

_____ (7) digital   G. 仪表灯

_____ (8) data   H. 紧急警示灯

_____ (9) dash light   I. 数据

_____ (10) hazard light   J. 外部的

_____ (11) tachometer   K. 照明

_____ (12) speedometer   L. 镜板

_____ (13) panel   M. 探照灯

_____ (14) instrument   N. 内部的

2. Choice（选择）

_____ (1) Technician A says that the lighting system provides power to both exterior and interior lights. Technician B says that the lighting system consists of the headlights, parking lights and taillights. Who is right?
    A. A only   B. B only
    C. both A and B   D. neither A nor B

_____ (2) Which of the following statements is not true?
    A. the lighting system consists of various control switches
    B. instrument panel mounts an array of electrical gauges
    C. the speedometer tells the vehicle speed
    D. an analog display is better for showing exact data

_____ (3) Which of the following statements about analog displays is not true?

    A. it is useful when the exact reading is important

    B. it is useful when the driver must see something quickly

    C. it is better for the tachometer

    D. none of the above

_____ (4) If you want to know the engine speed when you drive, which meter should you check?

    A. the odometer

    B. the tachometer

    C. the speedometer

    D. the kilometer

3. Translation（翻译）

(1) The lighting system provides power to both exterior and interior lights.

_____

(2) The speedometer tells the vehicle speed and the tachometer indicates engine speed.

_____

(3) Analog displays are useful when the driver must see something quickly and the exact reading is not important.

_____

(4) A digital display is better for showing exact data such as miles or operating hours.

_____

2.2.4 Power train system（传动系统）

1 Clutch（离合器）

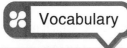

standard ['stændəd]　　adj. 标准的
locate [ləu'keit]　　　v. 位于
gradually　　　　　　adv. 逐渐地
['grædʒuəli]
eliminate [i'limineit]　v. 除去
abruptly [ə'brʌptli]　　adv. 突然地
connection　　　　　　n. 连接
[kə'nekʃn]
flywheel ['flaiwi:l]　　n. 飞轮
fork [fɔ:k]　　　　　　n. 叉
clamp [klæmp]　　　　v. 钳紧

1) Purpose of the clutch

All standard or manual transmissions have a clutch to engage or disengage the transmission. The clutch is located between the transmission and engine. If clutches were not used, every time the vehicle came to a stop, the engine would stop. The clutch engages the transmission gradually. This will eliminate jumping abruptly from no connection at all to a direct solid connection to the engine. See Fig.2-105.

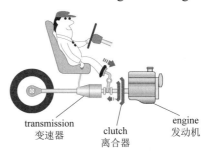

Fig.2-105　Clutch

2) The main parts of the clutch

Fig.2-106 shows the main parts of the clutch: the flywheel, clutch disc, pressure plate assembly, clutch release bearing and the clutch fork. When the clutch is disengaged, the flywheel and the pressure plate rotate independently. When the clutch is engaged, the pressure plate clamps the clutch disc to the flywheel, and the engine was connected to the transmission.

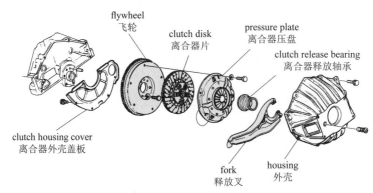

Fig.2-106　Clutch

3) Hydraulic clutch linkage

The hydraulic system consists of master cylinder and a slave cylinder. When the driver presses the clutch padel, hydraulic pressure is built up in the master cylinder. The pressure is sent through a tube into the slave cylinder. The slave cylinder piston movement is transmitted to the clutch fork, which disengages the clutch. Fig.2-107 shows the components of a hydraulic clutch linkage system.

Vocabulary	
slave cylinder	n. 分泵
tube [tju:b]	n. 管子

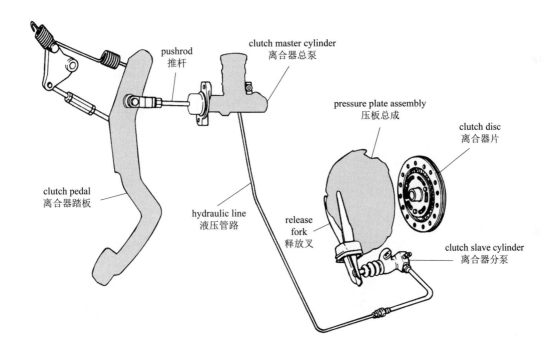

Fig.2-107　Hydraulic clutch linkage

★ Practice makes perfect （熟能生巧）

1. Match （对应）

_____ (1) standard	A. 位于……地点
_____ (2) locate	B. 轴承
_____ (3) flywheel	C. 逐渐地
_____ (4) bearing	D. 分泵
_____ (5) clamp	E. 连接
_____ (6) fork	F. 钳紧
_____ (7) gradually	G. 飞轮
_____ (8) connection	H. 标准的
_____ (9) abruptly	I. 叉子
_____ (10) eliminate	J. 突然地
_____ (11) slave cylinder	K. 管子
_____ (12) tube	L. 除去

2. Choice （选择）

_____ (1) The clutch is located between the transmission and the:
    A. engine
    B. wheels
    C. differential
    D. suspension

_____ (2) In order to eliminate jumping abruptly, the clutch must engage the transmission:
    A. abruptly
    B. suddenly
    C. gradually
    D. immediately

_____ (3) Which of the following parts is not included in the clutch?
   A. the clutch fork
   B. the flywheel
   C. the clutch disc
   D. the booster

_____ (4) When the clutch is engaged, the pressure plate clamps the clutch disc to the:
   A. release bearing
   B. release fork
   C. flywheel
   D. transmission

3. Translation（翻译）

(1) All standard or manual transmissions have a clutch to engage or disengage the transmission.

_____

(2) When the clutch is disengaged, the flywheel and the pressure plate rotate independently.

_____

(3) The slave cylinder piston movement is transmitted to the clutch fork, which disengages the clutch.

_____

(4) The hydraulic system consists of a master cylinder and a slave cylinder.

_____

2 Manual transmission(手动变速器)

Vocabulary

transmission [træns'miʃn]	n. 变速器
perform [pə'fɔ:m]	v. 执行
load [ləud]	v. 负载
reverse [ri'və:s]	v. 反向
neutral ['nju:trəl]	n. 空挡

1) Purpose of the transmission

Vehicles are required to perform under many types of loads. The transmission is designed to change the torque applied to driving wheels for different applications. In addition, the transmission is used to reverse the vehicle direction for parking and to provide neutral (no power) to the wheels. The manual transmission structure is shown in Fig.2-108.

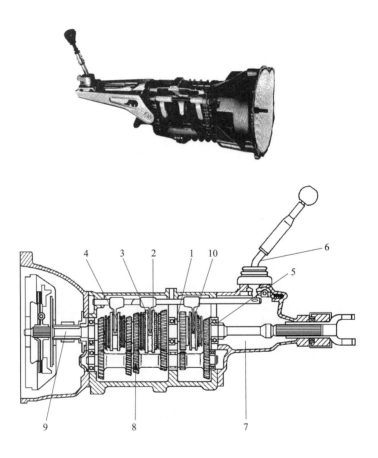

1-first-speed gear 一挡齿轮; 2-second-speed gear 二挡齿轮; 3-third-speed gear 三挡齿轮; 4-fourth-speed gear 四挡齿轮;
5-fifth-speed gear 五挡齿轮; 6-shift lever 变速杆; 7-main shaft 主轴(输出轴); 8-counter shaft 副轴;
9-clutch shaft 离合器轴; 10-reverse gear 倒挡齿轮

Fig.2-108 Manual transmission

2) Gear ratios

Gear ratios are determined by comparing the number of teeth on the output with the number of teeth on the input. As shown in Fig.2-109a), the gear ratio would be two to one, written 2:1. If both gears are the same size, then the speeds of both gears are equal. If the driving gear is smaller, the speed of the driven gear decreases. However, when the driving gear is larger, the speed of the driven gear increases. Fig.2-109 shows the speed ratio.

3) Transmission gears

The internal components of a transmission consist of a parallel set of metal shafts on which meshing gearsets of different ratios are mounted. By moving the shaft lever, gear ratios can be selected to generate different amounts of output torque and speed. Fig.2-110 shows a simplified view of a three-speed transmission.

> **Vocabulary**
>
> determine [di'tə:min]　　v. 决定
> driving ['draiviŋ]　　adj. 主动的
> driven ['drivn]　　adj. 被动的
> decrease [di'kri:s]　　v. 减少
> internal [in'tə:nəl]　　adj. 内部的
> parallel ['pærəlel]　　adj. 平行的
> mesh [meʃ]　　v. 啮合
> gearset ['giəset]　　n. 齿轮组
> select [si'lekt]　　v. 选择
> simplify ['simplifai]　　v. 简化

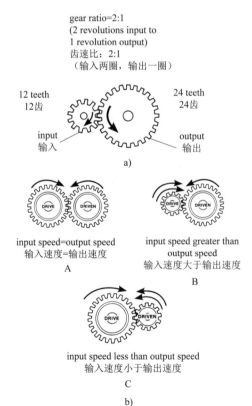

Fig.2-109　Gear ratios

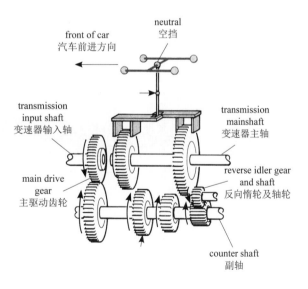

Fig.2-110　Transmission gears

★ Practice makes perfect（熟能生巧）

1. Match（对应）

_____ (1) perform   A. 变速器

_____ (2) reverse   B. 内部的

_____ (3) load   C. 齿轮组

_____ (4) neutral   D. 减少

_____ (5) driving   E. 反向

_____ (6) transmission   F. 啮合

_____ (7) internal   G. 负载

_____ (8) mesh   H. 空挡的

_____ (9) gearset   I. 被动的

_____ (10) driven   J. 简化

_____ (11) decrease   K. 执行

_____ (12) simplify   L. 主动的

2. Choice（选择）

_____ (1) The drive gear has 12 teeth and the driven gear has 24 teeth, the gear ratio would be:

     A. 2:1

     B. 24:12

     C. 1:2

     D. 12:24

_____ (2) Which of the following system can reverse the vehicle direction?

     A. suspension

     B. transmission

     C. cooling

     D. braking

_____ (3) Which one is not right?
　　　　　A. vehicles are required to perform under many types of loads
　　　　　B. the transmission is designed to change the torque applied to the driving wheels
　　　　　C. if the driving gear is larger, the speed of the driven gear decreases
　　　　　D. if the driving gear is smaller, the speed of the driven gear decreases

_____ (4) Which of the following system can change the torque applied to the driving wheels for different applications?
　　　　　A. suspension　　　　　B. lubrication
　　　　　C. transmission　　　　D. braking

3. Translation（翻译）

(1) The transmission is designed to change the torque applied to the driving wheels for different applications.

_____

(2) If the driving gear is smaller, the speed of the driven gear decreases.

_____

(3) By moving the shaft lever, gear ratios can be selected to generate different amounts of output torque and speed.

_____

(4) In addition, the transmission is used to reverse the vehicle direction for parking and to provide neutral to the wheels.

_____

3 Automatic transmission（自动变速器）

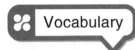

Vocabulary

factor ['fæktə(r)]	n.	因素
upshift ['ʌpʃift]	n.	升挡
downshift ['daunʃift]	n.	降挡
recently ['ri:sntli]	adv.	最近地
converter [kən'və:tə(r)]	n.	转换器
planetary ['plænətri]	adj.	行星的

1) Purpose of the automatic transmission

An automatic transmission selects gear ratios according to engine speed, powertrain load, vehicle speed and other operating factors. Shown in Fig.2-111. Little effort is needed on the part of the driver, because both upshifts and downshifts occur automatically. A driver-operated clutch is not needed to change gears. The most widely used automatic transmissions have three forward speeds and neutral, reverse and park arrangements. Until recently, all automatic transmissions were controlled by hydraulics. The torque converter connects the engine to the transmission gearing. The planetary gear system is used to produce the correct gear ratio for different torque and speed conditions. Various hydraulic controls are used to lock up parts of the gear system in an automatic transmission.

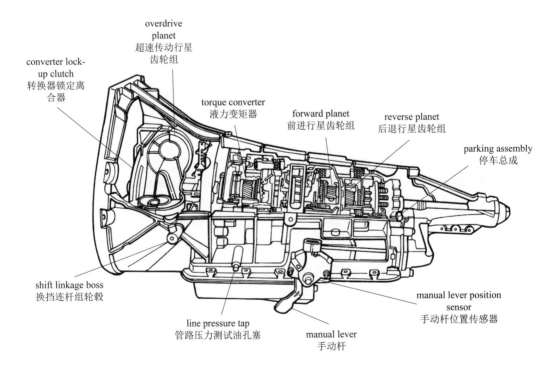

Fig.2-111 Automatic transmission

2) Torque converter

In the automatic transmission, a torque converter is used to engage and disengage the engine from the transmission. In Fig.2-112 a), a torque converter produces a fluid coupling in a manner similar to the operation of two fans.

Fig.2-112 b) shows the major parts of the torque converter. It includes the pump (also called impeller), the turbine and the stator. The stator is designed to improve oil circulation.

3) Planetary gears

The planetary gear system is used to produce different gear ratios. It is a circular gearset with three distinct elements: (1) a central or sun gear, (2) three or four planet gears which rotate around the sun gear, and (3) an internally toothed ring gear which rotates around the planet gears. The gearset ratios can be varied by stopping any one element and allowing the other two elements to rotate. As shown in Fig.2-113.

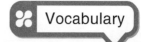

Vocabulary	
coupling ['kʌplɪŋ]	n. 耦合器
manner ['mænə(r)]	n. 方式
similar ['sɪmələ(r)]	adj. 类似的
impeller [ɪm'pelə]	n. 泵轮
turbine ['tɜːbaɪn]	n. 涡轮
circulation [ˌsɜːkjə'leɪʃn]	n. 循环

Vocabulary

circular ['sɜːkjələ(r)]	adj. 圆形的
distinct [dɪs'tɪŋkt]	adj. 不同的
sun gear	n. 太阳轮
planet gear	n. 行星齿轮
internally [ɪn'tɜːnəli]	adv. 内部地

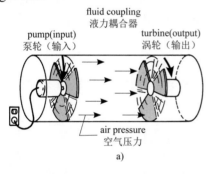

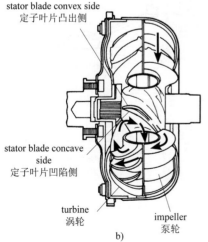

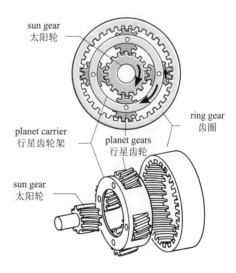

Fig.2-112 Torque converter

Fig.2-113 Planetary gear

Gear combinations

GEAR COMBINATIONS				
GEAR	RING	CARRIER	SUN	SPEED CHANGE (INPUT TO OUTPUT)
1	OUTPUT	INPUT	HOLD	INCREASE
2	HOLD	INPUT	OUTPUT	INCREASE
3	INPUT	OUTPUT	HOLD	LOWER
4	HOLD	OUTPUT	INPUT	LOWER
5	INPUT	HOLD	OUTPUT	INCREASE REVERSE
6	OUTPUT	HOLD	INPUT	LOWER REVERSE
7	HOLD ANY TWO GEARS			DIRECT DRIVE
8	LOWER REVERSE			NEUTRAL

4) Hydraulic control system

The automatic transmission is controlled by the hydraulic system. When the operator shifts into drive, low, reverse, or any other gear, hydraulic pressure is used to lock up different clutches and bands on the planetary gear system. The torque converter also uses transmission fluid. See Fig.2-114.

The ATF (automatic transmission fluid) lubricates the high friction points of the transmission to prevent overheating and wear.

Vocabulary

band [bænd]　　　　　　　　　　n. 带
ATF　　　　　　　　　　　n.自动变速器油

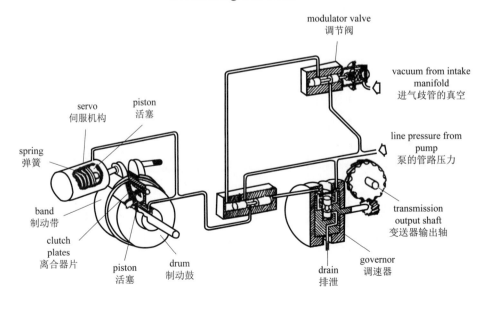

Fig.2-114　Hydraulic control system

★ Practice makes perfect （熟能生巧）

1. Match（对应）

_____ (1) upshift   A. 行星的

_____ (2) converter   B. 循环

_____ (3) planetary   C. 泵轮

_____ (4) circulation   D. 太阳轮

_____ (5) turbine   E. 圆形的

_____ (6) impeller   F. 带

_____ (7) coupling   G. 自动变速器油

_____ (8) ATF   H. 耦合器

_____ (9) band   I. 涡轮

_____ (10) downshift   J. 内部地

_____ (11) circular   K. 升挡

_____ (12) sun gear   L. 降挡

_____ (13) internally   M. 不同的

_____ (14) distinct   N. 转换器

2. Choice（选择）

_____ (1) An automatic transmission selects gear ratios according to the:
　　A. engine speed
　　B. power train load
　　C. vehicle speed
　　D. all of the above

_____ (2) Which of the following in the automatic transmission is used to engage and disengage the engine from the transmission?
　　A. the torque converter
　　B. the clutch
　　C. the planetary gear system
　　D. the hydraulic system

_____ (3) Which of the following is used to produce different gear ratios?
　　　　　　A. the torque converter
　　　　　　B. the clutch
　　　　　　C. the planetary gear system
　　　　　　D. the hydraulic system
_____ (4) The automatic transmission is controlled by the hydraulic system. What is the fluid used in the hydraulic system?
　　　　　　A. ABS
　　　　　　B. ATF
　　　　　　C. BMP
　　　　　　D. APG

3. Translation (翻译)

(1) The most widely used automatic transmissions have three forward speeds and neutral, reverse and park arrangements.

_____

(2) In the automatic transmission, a torque converter is used to engage and disengage the engine from the transmission.

_____

(3) The planetary gear system is used to produce different gear ratios.

_____

(4) The ATF lubricates the high friction points of the transmission to prevent overheating and wear.

_____

4 Drive shaft assembly（传动轴组成）

1) Purpose of the drive shaft assembly

The drive shaft is used to transmit the power from the engine and transmission to the differential and axles on rear-wheel drive vehicles. The drive shaft must also be designed to allow shortening or lengthening between the differential and transmission. As shown in Fig.2-115.

2) Universal joint

The universal joint, also called U-joint, allows two rotating shafts to operate at different angles. See Fig.2-116. The universal joint is made of several parts. The center of the universal joint is called the cross and bearing assembly. The yokes are attached directly to the drive shaft. Four bearing caps are placed on the universal joint. Fig.2-116b) shows an exploded view of a Cardan universal joint.

> **Vocabulary**
>
> differential [ˌdifə'renʃl]   n. 差速器
> shorten ['ʃɔ:tn]   v. 缩短
> lengthen ['leŋθən]   v. 伸长
> universal joint   n. 万向节
> cross [krɔs]   n. 十字轴
> yoke [jəuk]   n. 轭
> attach [ə'tætʃ]   v. 附着
> explode [ik'spləud]   v. 爆炸

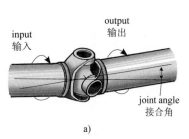

a)

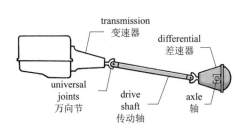

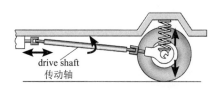

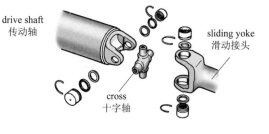

b)

Fig.2-115 Drive shaft assembly   Fig.2-116 Universal joint

Vocabulary

hollow ['hɔləu]　　adj. 中空的
carbon ['kɑ:bən]　　n. 碳
steel [sti:l]　　n. 钢
torsional ['tɔ:ʃənəl]　　adj. 扭转的
bending ['bendiŋ]　　adj. 弯曲的
irregular [i'regjələ(r)]　　adj. 不规则的
surface ['sə:fis]　　n. 表面
spline [splain]　　n. 花键

3) Drive shaft construction

The drive shaft is made of a hollow carbon steel tube. Fig.2-117a) shows the parts of a standard drive shaft. In most cases, two universal joints are placed on both sides. The most common location for the slip joint is on the output of the transmission. On certain vehicles, the slip joint is located at the center of the drive shaft. The drive shaft must have a high resistance against the torsional or bending forces. See Fig.2-117b).

4) Slip joint

The slip joint is designed to allow the drive shaft to be shorten or lengthen when the car goes over an irregular road surface. The slip joint is usually composed of internal and external splines. It is located on the front end of the drive shaft and connected to the transmission. Shown in Fig.2-118.

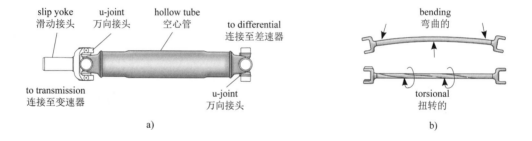

Fig.2-117　Drive shaft construction

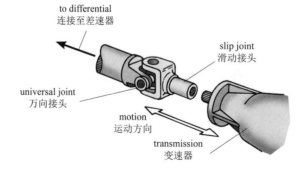

Fig.2-118　Slip joint

★ Practice makes perfect（熟能生巧）

1. Match（对应）

_____ (1) differential   A. 缩短
_____ (2) lengthen   B. 十字轴
_____ (3) universal joint   C. 轭
_____ (4) yoke   D. 不规则的
_____ (5) cross   E. 中空的
_____ (6) explode   F. 伸长
_____ (7) spline   G. 差速器
_____ (8) irregular   H. 爆炸
_____ (9) hollow   I. 万向节
_____ (10) shorten   J. 扭转的
_____ (11) carbon   K. 栓槽
_____ (12) torsional   L. 碳
_____ (13) bending   M. 弯曲的

2. Choice（选择）

_____ (1) Technician A says that the drive shaft must be designed to allow for up and down motion on the differential. Technician B says that the drive shaft is used to generate the power. Who is right?
　　　A. A only　　　　　　　　B. B only
　　　C. both A and B　　　　　D. neither A nor B

_____ (2) Which of the following can allow two rotating shafts to operate At different angles?
　　　A. the bearing
　　　B. the universal joint
　　　C. the planetary gear system
　　　D. the flywheel

_____ (3) The slip joint is usually composed of internal and external:

    A. gear

    B. ring gear

    C. splines

    D. pin

_____ (4) Which of the following statements is not true?

    A. the drive shaft is made of a hollow carbon steel tube

    B. the U-joint can allow the drive shaft to be shorten and lengthen

    C. the drive shaft must have a high resistance against torsional force

    D. none of the above

3. Translation（翻译）

(1) The drive shaft is used to transmit the power from the engine and transmission to the differential and axles on rear-wheel drive vehicles.

_____

(2) The universal joint allows two rotating shafts to operate at different angles.

_____

(3) The drive shaft must have a high resistance against torsional or bending forces.

_____

(4) The slip joint is designed to allow the drive shaft to be shorten and lengthen.

_____

5 Differential（差速器）

1) Functions of the differential

The differential actually performs several functions. See Fig.2-119.

(1) Differentiation: Allows the wheel on the outside of a turn to rotate faster than the wheel on the inside to prevent tires scrubbing.

(2) Limited-slip: When the vehicle runs on a slippery surface, the limited-slip differential can avoid wheels slipping.

(3) Gear reduction: Provides a gear reduction, or a torque multiplication.

2) Differential main parts

Fig.2-120 shows the main parts of the differential:

(1) Drive pinion: It is the main input shaft to the differential.

(2) Ring gear: Its purpose is to drive the remaining parts of the differential.

(3) Differential case: It holds several bevel gears.

(4) Two differential side gears and two pinion gears: All four gears are meshed together.

(5) Axle: The axles are attached to the differential side gear, causing the vehicle to move.

Vocabulary

differentiation [ˌdɪfəˌrenʃɪ'eɪʃn]	n. 差速器
outside [ˌaut'saɪd]	n. 外部
scrub [skrʌb]	v. 擦、刷
slippery ['slɪpəri]	adj. 湿滑的
redirect [ˌriːdə'rekt]	v. 改方向
multiplication [ˌmʌltɪplɪ'keɪʃn]	n. 增加
case [keɪs]	n. 外壳
hold [həʊld]	v. 持有
bevel gear	n. 斜齿轮

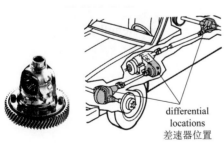

Fig.2-119　Differential

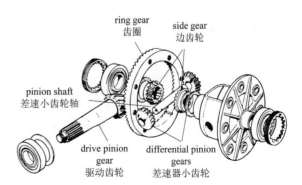

Fig.2-120　Differential main parts

Vocabulary

additional [əˈdiʃənl]	adj. 附加的
preload spring	n. 预负荷弹簧
rub [rʌb]	v. 摩擦
exact [igˈzækt]	adj. 正确的
combine [kəmˈbain]	v. 结合
transaxle [ˈtrænˌsæksəl]	n. 联合传动器
viscosity [visˈkɔsiti]	n. 黏度
damage [ˈdæmidʒ]	v. 损坏
lack [læk]	n. 缺乏

3) Limited slip differential (LSD)

The limited slip differential can prevent one wheel from spinning more rapidly than the other. Fig.2-121 shows the LSD system. There are three additional parts:

(1) Clutch plate: It is used to lock up both wheels.

(2) Preload spring: It is used to produce the pressure against the clutches.

(3) Pressure ring: It is a surface against which the clutches rub for the side gear.

4) Differential lubrication

The differential uses several types of lubricants. The exact type depends on the year of the vehicle and whether the differential is separate or combined into the transaxle. Also, the viscosity will vary with the weather condition. Look at Fig.2-122, this pinion gear was damaged for lack of lubrication in the differential.

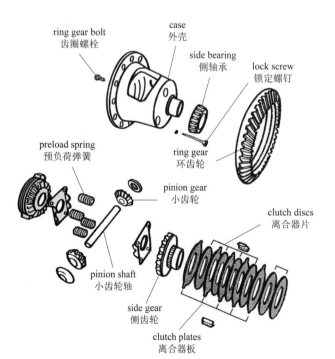

Fig.2-121 LSD

Fig.2-122 Damaged pinion gear due to lack of lubrication

★ Practice makes perfect（熟能生巧）

1. Match（对应）

_____ (1) slippery   A. 差速
_____ (2) redirect   B. 外部
_____ (3) case   C. 擦
_____ (4) differentiation   D. 湿滑的
_____ (5) bevel gear   E. 外壳
_____ (6) additional   F. 预负荷弹簧
_____ (7) outside   G. 联合传动器
_____ (8) combine   H. 斜齿轮
_____ (9) preload spring   I. 附加的
_____ (10) scrub   J. 结合
_____ (11) transaxle   K. 黏度
_____ (12) viscosity   L. 损坏
_____ (13) damage   M. 改方向

2. Choice（选择）

_____ (1) Which of these is not the function of the differential?
　　　　　A. torque increasing
　　　　　B. differentiation
　　　　　C. limited-slip
　　　　　D. gear reduction

_____ (2) Which of the following is the main input shaft to the differential?
　　　　　A. differential case
　　　　　B. ring gear
　　　　　C. drive pinion
　　　　　D. axle

_____ (3) Which of the following can prevent one wheel from spinning more rapidly than the other?

   A. differential
   B. LSD
   C. drive pinion
   D. u-joint

_____ (4) Which of the following can produce the pressure against the clutches?

   A. the preload spring
   B. the clutch plate
   C. the pressure ring
   D. the cross

3. Translation（翻译）

(1) When the vehicle runs on a slippery surface, the limited-slip differential can avoid wheels to slipping.

(2) The purpose of the ring gear is to drive the remaining parts of the differential.

(3) The limited slip differential can prevent one wheel from spinning more rapidly than the other.

(4) The Preload spring is used to produce the pressure against the clutches.

2.2.5 Emission control systems（废气控制系统）

1 Vehicle emissions（汽车废气）

1) Types of pollutants

Three kinds of emissions that are being controlled in gasoline engines today are HC (unburned hydrocarbons), CO (carbon monoxide), and NO_x (oxides of nitrogen). Unburned hydrocarbons emitted by the automobile are largely unburned portions of fuel. Carbon monoxide emissions are increased as the combustion process becomes less efficient. NO_x is the principal chemical that causes smog. See Fig.2-123.

2) Hydrocarbon (HC)

Unburned hydrocarbons are particles, usually meansvapor of gasoline that have not been burned during combustion. They are present in the exhaust and crankcase vapor. Most hydrocarbons are poisonous at concentration above several hundred parts per million (PPM). Hydrocarbons are the main ingredient of photochemical smog. See Fig.2-124.

Vocabulary

emission [i'miʃən]	n. 废气
pollutant [pə'lu:tnt]	n. 污染物
hydrocarbon [ˌhaidrə'kɑ:bən]	n. 碳氢化合物
carbon monoxide	n. 一氧化碳
oxide ['ɔksaid]	n. 氧化物
nitrogen ['naitrədʒən]	n. 氮
portion ['pɔ:ʃən]	n. 部分
principal ['prinsəpəl]	adj. 主要的
chemical ['kemikl]	n. 化学物质
vapor ['veipə]	n. 蒸气
present ['preznt]	adj. 在场的
poisonous ['pɔizənəs]	adj. 有毒的
concentration [ˌkɔnsn'treiʃn]	n. 浓度
parts per million	n. 百万分之一
ingredient [in'gri:diənt]	n. 成分
photochemical [ˌfəutə'kemikəl]	adj. 光化学的
smog [smɔg]	n. 烟雾

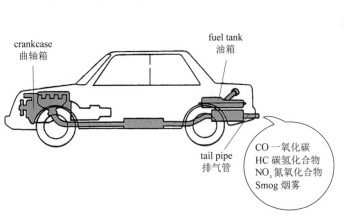

Fig.2-123 Types of pollutants

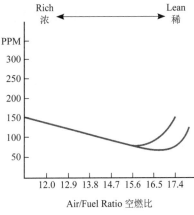

Fig.2-124 Hydrocarbon (HC)

Vocabulary

deadly ['dedli]	adj. 致命的
colorless ['kʌləlis]	adj. 无色的
odorless ['əudəlis]	adj. 无臭的
inhale [in'heil]	v. 吸入
quantity ['kwɔntəti]	n. 数量
vision ['viʒn]	n. 视力
extreme [ik'stri:m]	adj. 极度的
temperature ['temprəitʃə(r)]	n. 温度
oxygen ['ɔksidʒən]	n. 氧气
greenhouse ['gri:nhaus]	n. 温室

3) Carbon monoxide (CO)

CO is considered a deadly poison gas that is colorless and odorless. When people inhale CO in small quantity, it causes headaches and vision difficulties. In larger quantities, it causes sleepiness and in many cases, death. CO emissions are increased as the combustion process becomes less efficient. Thus whenever the engine operates in a rich air-fuel mixture, increasing CO is the result. Shown in Fig.2-125.

4) Nitrogen oxides (NO_x)

Nitrogen oxides (NO_x) form freely under extreme heat conditions. When the combustion temperature reaches 1090℃ to 1370℃, the nitrogen and oxygen in the air-fuel mixture combine to form large quantities of nitrogen oxides, Fig.2-126. NO_x is the main chemical that causes smog. NO_x is also considered a major greenhouse gas.

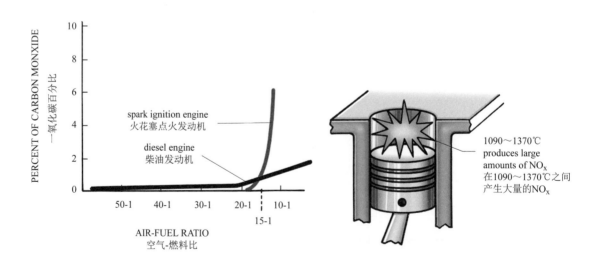

Fig.2-125　CO　　　　　　　　　　　　Fig.2-126　NO_x

5) Emission control

The best method of reducing the emission of nitrogen oxides is to reduce the temperature of the combustion process. Doing this, however, will result in less-efficient burning and increase in HC and CO emissions. Whenever steps are taken to reduce HC and CO emissions, NO_x emissions increase. It is very important to keep the air-fuel ratio close to 14.7 to 1 for more effective emission control, Fig.2-127.

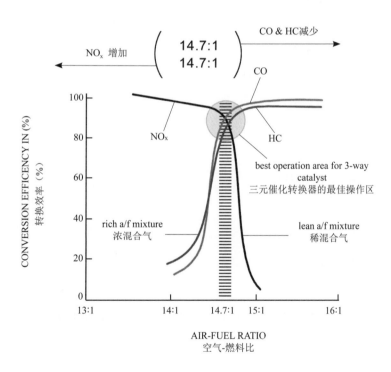

Fig.2-127　Emission control

★ Practice makes perfect（熟能生巧）

1. Match（对应）

_____ (1) emission   A. 污染物

_____ (2) carbon monoxide   B. 吸入

_____ (3) oxide   C. 无色的

_____ (4) inhale   D. 一氧化碳

_____ (5) pollutant   E. 有毒的

_____ (6) colorless   F. 氧化物

_____ (7) parts per million G. 有效的

_____ (8) concentration   H. 烟雾

_____ (9) poisonous   I. 光化学的

_____ (10) hydrocarbon   J. 部分

_____ (11) effective   K. 废气

_____ (12) smog   L. 化学物质

_____ (13) photochemical   M. 碳氢化合物

_____ (14) portion   N. 浓度

_____ (15) chemical   O. 百万分之一

2. Choice（选择）

_____ (1) Which of these is not the harmful chemical of vehicle emissions?

　　A. CO　　　B. CO_2　　　C. NO_x　　　D. HC

_____ (2) Three kinds of emissions that are being controlled in gasoline engines today are:

　　A. CO、HC、NO_x　　　B. HO、CO、NO_x

　　C. CO、HO、CO　　　　D. CO、HC、NO_x

_____ (3) When the combustion process becomes less efficient, CO emissions are:

　　A. decreased　　　B. increased

　　C. lighter　　　　D. not changed

_____ (4) Which of the following statements about vehicle emissions is wrong?
  A. NO_x is the principle chemical that causes smog
  B. NO_x is also considered a major greenhouse gas
  C. CO is not a deadly poison gas
  D. HC is the main ingredient of photochemical smog

_____ (5) For more effective emission control, it is very important to keep the air-fuel ratio close to :
  A. 14.7 to 1   B. 17.4 to 1
  C. 7.4 to 1   D. 4.7 to 1

3. Translation (翻译)

(1) Hydrocarbons are the main ingredient of photochemical smog.

_____

(2) When people inhale CO in larger quantities, it causes sleepiness and in many cases, death.

_____

(3) Nitrogen oxides form freely under extreme heat conditions.

_____

(4) It is very important to keep the air-fuel ratio close to (14) 7 to 1 for more effective emission control.

_____

2 Emission control systems（车辆废气控制系统）

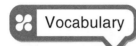

Vocabulary

ventilation [ˌventiˈleiʃən]	n. 通风	
blow-by gas	n. 吹漏气	
atmosphere [ˈætməsfiə(r)]	n. 大气	
scavenge [ˈskævindʒ]	v. 排除废气	
dilute [daiˈluːt]	v. 稀释	
benefit [ˈbenifit]	v. 有益于	
eliminate [iˈlimineit]	v. 清除	
harmful [ˈhɑːmful]	adj. 有害的	
inlet [ˈinlet]	n. 进入	
warm [wɔːm]	v. 温暖	
warm up	v. 热车	
duct [dʌkt]	n. 管	
bimetal [baiˈmetl]	n. 双金属	
modulator [ˈmɔdjuleitə]	n. 调节器	

1) Positive crankcase ventilation (PCV)

The PCV system has two major functions. It prevents the emission of blow-by gases from the engine crankcase to the atmosphere. It also scavenges the crankcase vapor that could dilute the oil. The PCV system benefits the vehicle's driveability by eliminating harmful crankcase gases, reducing air pollution and promoting fuel economy. See Fig.2-128.

2) Heated air inlet

This system controls the temperature of the air on its way to the carburetor or fuel injection body. By warming the air, it reduces HC and CO emissions by improved fuel vaporization and faster warm up. The heated air inlet system includes:

(1) Heated air inlet duct.
(2) Air inlet door vacuum motor.
(3) Air cleaner bimetal sensor.
(4) Cold weather modulator.

As shown in Fig.2-129.

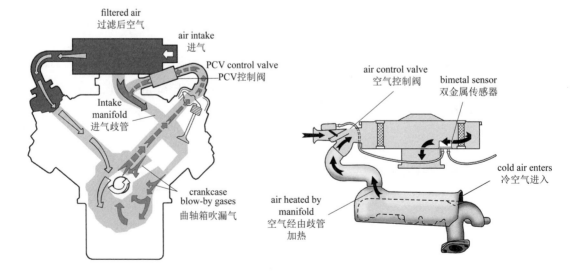

Fig.2-128　PCV System　　　　Fig.2-129　Heated air inlet

3) Exhaust gas recirculation (EGR)

Vehicles are equipped with EGR systems to reduce NO_x emissions. In operation, part of the exhaust gas (usually less than 10%) is sent back through the intake manifold. The exhaust gases, which are considerably cooler than the combustion temperature, cool down the process of combustion. Normally, the EGR system operates when the engine is at high speed. Shown in Fig.2-130.

4) Air injection system

A typical air injection system injects air (oxygen) directly into the exhaust flow. Shown in Fig.2-131. Oxygen in the air combines with the HC and CO to continue the burning that reduces the HC and CO concentrations. This method of cleaning the exhaust does not affect the efficiency of combustion. However, a small amount of horsepower (up to 3 Hp) is needed to operate the air injection pump.

Vocabulary

recirculation [ri:ˌsə:kjə'leiʃn]	n. 再循环
considerably [kən'sidərəbli]	adv. 相当地
normally ['nɔ:məli]	adj. 通常地
flow [fləu]	n. 流量
affect [ə'fekt]	v. 影响
efficiency [i'fiʃnsi]	n. 效率

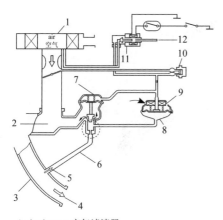

1-air cleaner 空气滤清器；
2-intake manifold 进气歧管；
3-exhaust pipe 排气管；
4-exhaust gas 排出气体；
5-recycle exhaust gas 回流废气；
6-EGR tube 废气回收管；
7-EGR control valve 废气回收控制阀；
8-BPT valve 排压控制阀；
9-atmospheric pressure 大气压力；
10-thermal vacuum valve 热真空阀；
11-vacuum solenoid valve 真空电磁阀；
12-to distributor 至分电器

Fig.2-130 EGR System

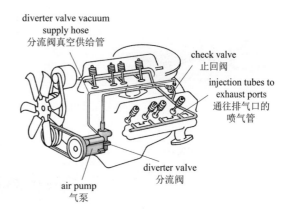

Fig.2-131 Air injection system

Vocabulary

catalytic [kætə'litik]	n. 催化剂
platinum ['plætinəm]	n. 铂
coat [kəut]	v. 涂膜
honeycomb ['hʌnikəum]	n. 蜂巢
react [ri'ækt]	v. 反应
formation [fɔ:'meiʃən]	n. 形成
dioxide [dai'ɔksaid]	n. 二氧化物
rhodium ['rəudiəm]	n. 铑
introduce [ˌintrə'dju:s]	v. 介绍
charcoal ['tʃɑ:kəul]	n. 活性炭
canister ['kænistə(r)]	n. 罐

5) Catalytic converter

Catalytic converters are the most effective devices for controlling exhaust emissions. When exhaust gases are passing through a platinum coated honeycomb core, the HC and CO react with the oxygen in the air. The result is the formation of water and carbon dioxide. When the metal rhodium is used as the catalyst, the NO_x in the exhaust gases is transformed to harmless nitrogen and oxygen. Shown in Fig.2-132.

6) Evaporative emission control system

As shown in Fig.2-133, this system reduces HC emissions by drawing fuel vapor from the fuel tank and the carburetor bowl and introduces them into the intake air to be burned. The most obvious part of the system is the charcoal canister. When the engine is not running, the charcoal canister stores fuel vapor. When the vehicle is restarted, vapor in the canister are drawn by the engine cylinder vacuum into the intake manifold to be burned in the engine.

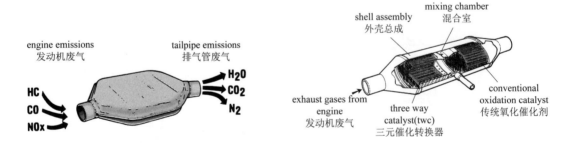

Fig.2-132 Catalytic converter

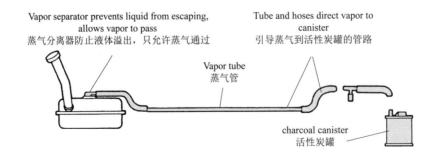

Fig.2-133 Evaporative emission control system

★ Practice makes perfect（熟能生巧）

1. Match（对应）

_____ (1) ventilation   A. 排除废气

_____ (2) harmful   B. 稀释

_____ (3) scavenge   C. 热车

_____ (4) dilute   D. 再循环

_____ (5) recirculation   E. 通风

_____ (6) warm up   F. 双金属

_____ (7) bimetal   G. 有害的

_____ (8) catalytic   H. 催化剂

_____ (9) platinum   I. 二氧化物

_____ (10) honeycomb   J. 活性炭

_____ (11) dioxide   K. 罐

_____ (12) charcoal   L. 蜂巢

_____ (13) canister   M. 白金

2. Choice（选择）

_____ (1) Which of these is the function of the PCV system?
      A. it scavenges the crankcase of vapor
      B. it can reduce air pollution and promote fuel economy
      C. it can eliminate harmful crankcase gases
      D. all of the above

_____ (2) Which of the following parts is not included in the heated air inlet system?
      A. heated air outlet duct   B. air inlet door vacuum motor
      C. air cleaner bimetal sensor   D. cold weather modulator

_____ (3) What is the function of the exhaust gas recirculation (EGR) system?
      A. to reduce HC emissions   B. to reduce NO_x emissions
      C. to reduce CO emissions   D. to reduce HC emissions

_____ (4) Which of the following statements about emission control systems is wrong?
　　A. the PCV system can eliminate harmful crankcase gases
　　B. the EGR system can reduce NO_x emissions
　　C. normally, the EGR system operates when the engine is at low speed
　　D. the catalytic converter can control exhaust emissions well

_____ (5) Which of the following systems can reduce HC emissions by drawing fuel vapor from the fuel tank?
　　A. the PCV system
　　B. the EGR system
　　C. the air injection system
　　D. the evaporative emission control system

_____ (6) The catalytic converter can change exhaust gases into:
　　A. water and CO　　　　B. CO and CO_2
　　C. water and CO_2　　　D. CO and HC

3. Translation（翻译）

(1) The PCV system benefits the vehicle's driveability by eliminating harmful crankcase gases, reducing air pollution and promoting fuel economy.

_____

(2) By warming up the air, it reduces HC and CO emissions by improved fuel vaporization and faster warm up.

_____

(3) Normally, the EGR system operates when the engine is at high speed.

_____

(4) A typical air injection system injects air (oxygen) directly into the exhaust flow.

_____

(5) Catalytic converters are the most effective devices for controlling exhaust emissions.

_____

2.3　New energy automobile drive system（新能源汽车动力系统）

1 Power battery pack（动力蓄电池组）

The power battery pack is one of the core systems of new energy vehicles, which provides the power source for the whole system. Through the control system, the power stored in the battery is supplied to the motor to drive the wheel. Shown in Fig.2-134.

At present, the mainstream electric vehicles use lithium batteries as power batteries. The power battery pack is generally installed in the lower part of the vehicle body, and generally consists of power battery box, power battery module, power battery system BMS, thermal management system and other auxiliary components. Shown in Fig.2-135.

Vocabulary

pack [pæk]	n. 包；箱
provide [prə'vaɪd]	v. 提供
rotate ['routeɪt]	v. 转动
lithium ['lɪθiəm]	n. 锂
module ['mɑ:dʒu:l]	n. 模块
generally ['dʒenrəli]	adv. 通常的
thermal ['θɜːrml]	adj. 热量的
management ['mænɪdʒmənt]	n. 管理
auxiliary [ɔːg'zɪliəri]	adj. 辅助的
switch [swɪtʃ]	n. 开关
voltage ['voʊltɪdʒ]	n. 电压
interface ['ɪntərfeɪs]	n. 接口
tube [tu:b]	n. 管

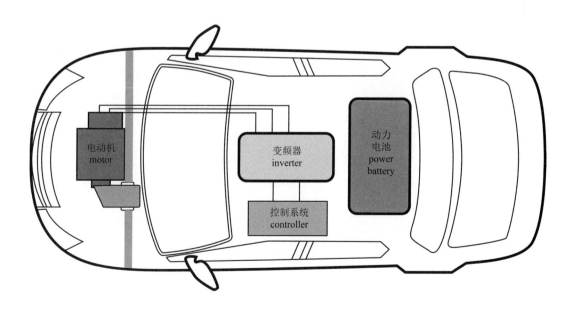

Fig.2-134　Electric vehicle power system

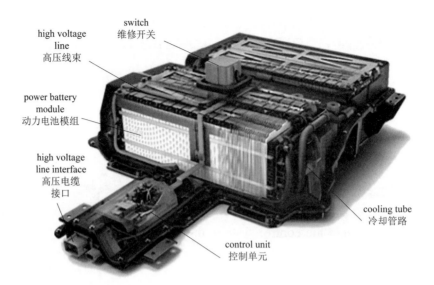

Fig.2-135　Power battery pack

★ Practice makes perfect（熟能生巧）

1. Match（对应）

_____ (1) auxiliary   A. 电压
_____ (2) switch   B. 接口
_____ (3) lithium   C. 管
_____ (4) pack   D. 控制单元
_____ (5) interface   E. 辅助的
_____ (6) voltage   F. 锂
_____ (7) module   G. 转动
_____ (8) tube   H. 箱
_____ (9) rotate   I. 模块

2. Choice（选择）

_____ (1) Which of these provides energy for vehicles?
    A. power battery   B. motor
    C. controller   D. reducer

_____ (2) Where is the power battery usually installed?
    A. on top of the vehicle body
    B. in the lower part of the vehicle body
    C. in front of the vehicle body
    D. in the engine compartment

_____ (3) Which is the most commonly used power battery on new energy vehicles?
    A. lead-acid battery   B. lithium battery
    C. solar battery   D. fuel cell

_____ (4) Which of the following is not a part of a power battery?
    A. thermal management system   B. power battery box
    C. power battery module   D. power motor

3. Translation (翻译)

(1) Through the control system, the power stored in the battery is supplied to the motor to drive the wheel.

---

(2) At present, the mainstream electric vehicles use lithium batteries as power batteries.

---

(3) The power battery pack is generally installed in the lower part of the vehicle body.

---

2 Electric motor and Reducer（电动机和减速器）

1) Electric motor

Electric motor is a device that converts the electric energy of power battery into mechanical energy. At present, the motors used in new energy vehicles include DC brush motor, brushless direct current motor (BLDCM), induction motor and switched reluctance motor. All motors are mainly composed of stator and rotor. See Fig.2-136.

Vocabulary

device [dɪ'vaɪs]　　　　n. 装置
convert [kən'vɜːrt]　　　v. 转换
mechanical [mə'kænɪkl] adj. 机械的
brush [brʌʃ]　　　　　 n. 刷子
direct [də'rekt]　　　　 adj. 直接的
current ['kɜːrənt]　　　 n. 电流
induction [ɪn'dʌkʃn] n. 催生、感应
reluctance [rɪ'lʌktəns]　 n. 磁阻

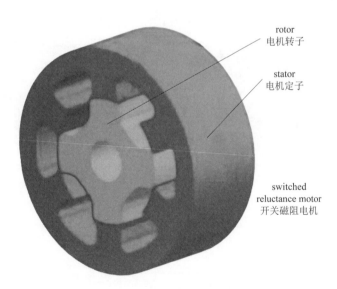

Fig.2-136　Motor structure

Vocabulary

reducer [rəˈdusər]	n. 减速器
function [ˈfʌŋkʃn]	n. 作用
torque [tɔːrk]	n. 转矩
gear [ɡɪr]	n. 齿轮
shaft [ʃæft]	n. 轴

2) Reducer

The main function of the reducer is to reduce the speed of the drive motor and increase the torque of the drive motor. The reducer is mainly composed of jackshaft input gear, jackshaft output gear, output shaft gear, input gear, parking motor and parking pawl. Fig.2-137 shows the structure of reducer.

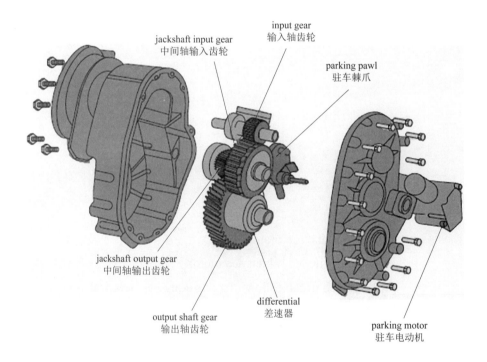

Fig.2-137　Reducer structure

★ Practice makes perfect（熟能生巧）

1. Match（对应）

_____ (1) brush   A. 磁阻

_____ (2) current   B. 转矩

_____ (3) convert   C. 减速器

_____ (4) reluctance   D. 电流

_____ (5) torque   E. 轴

_____ (6) reducer   F. 齿轮

_____ (7) shaft   G. 作用

_____ (8) gear   H. 转换

_____ (9) function   I. 感应

_____ (10) induction   J. 刷子

2. Choice（选择）

_____ (1) Which is not the driving motor of new energy vehicles?

    A. DC brush motor

    B. magnetic stepping motor

    C. induction motor

    D. switched reluctance motor

_____ (2) Which of the following parts converts electrical energy into mechanical energy?

    A. motor   B. battery

    C. reducer   D. gear

_____ (3) Which of the following is not a retarder function?

    A. reduce the speed of the drive motor

    B. increase the torque of the drive motor

    C. transfer power

    D. provide the energy

3. Translation（翻译）

(1) Electric motor is a device that converts the electric energy of power battery into mechanical energy.

(2) All motors are mainly composed of stator and rotor.

(3) The main function of the reducer is to reduce the speed of the drive motor and increase the torque of the drive motor.

Unit 3　Automobile Applied English
单元 3　汽车应用英语

3.1　Basic dialogue
（英语基本会话篇）

3.1.1　Customer's reception
（接待顾客）

Good morning.
早上好。

Can/May I help you, Sir/Madam?
你好，这位（先生、女士）有什么可以帮忙的吗？

What can I do for you, Sir/Madam?
你好，我能帮这位（先生、女士）做些什么呢？

Please wait a minute.
请稍等一下。

Pardon?I beg your pardon? Excuse me.
什么？请问你说什么？打扰一下。

The weather is very nice today.
今天的天气非常好。

Do you understand?
你明白吗？

Would you book this car?
您要预定这台车吗？

What's wrong?
怎么了？

Where is your car?
你的车在哪里？

What's wrong with your car?
你的车怎么了？

Is your engine working well?
你的发动机工作正常吗？

It will take three days to repair.
修理需要三天的时间。

Something wrong with your suspension system.
你的悬架系统出问题了。

How much does it cost?
这个多少钱？

These are the details. This is the detailed account.
这些是修车的具体明细，这是具体账目。

Cash or card?

现金还是刷卡？

Please sign here.

请在这签名。

Here is your receipt.

这是您的收据。

When will you come?

您什么时候来？

Your car will be ready today.

你的车今天就会准备好。

3.1.2 Answer terms
（回答用语）

I see.

我知道了。

I got it.

我知道了。

I can understand.

我能理解。

I can't believe it.

简直无法让人相信。

Are you kidding?/Are you joking?

你开玩笑呢吧？

Great! Fantastic!

太棒了！太酷了！

That's too bad.

那太糟糕了。

Sorry to hear that.

很遗憾听到它。

Glad to hear that.

很高兴听到它。

Sure.

当然！

Certainly.

当然！

Of course.

当然！

That's all right.

好吧。

No problem.

没有问题。

Never mind.

别介意。

I hope so.

我希望如此。

Let me see.

让我看看。

How should I say?

我应该怎么说？

Frankly speaking, …

坦率地说，……

How about/What about…?

……怎么样？

I'm afraid so.

恐怕如此吧。

I don't think so.

我不这么认为。

I'm afraid not.

恐怕不行。

I hope not.

希望不是这样。

I disagree with you.

我不同意你的观点。

I agree with you.

我同意你的观点。

I totally agree with you.

我完全赞同你的看法。

That's a good idea.

那个主意很棒。

That's a bad idea.

这个主意不怎么样。

You're welcome.

不客气。

Will you/Would you like to…?

你想……？

Why don't you…?

你为什么不……？

What do you think about that repair shop?

你觉得那家修车行怎么样？

What do you think about that mechanic?

你觉得那个技师怎么样？

Would you like to have a regular check-up?

你想做定期检查吗？

Would you like to have a regular maintenance?

你想给你的车做定期保养吗？

Why don't you come in and see the detailed information?

你为什么不进来看看详细的信息呢？

3.1.3 Customers reception by phone
（电话接待客人）

Madam: Can/May I speak to Mr. Shi?
我能跟史先生通话吗？

Sir: Who's speaking?

你是哪里？

Madam: This is Sanlitun Car Shop.
我们是三里屯汽车店。

Sir: Sorry, he is out.
抱歉，他没在。

Madam: Oh, I see and I will call him later.
哦，我一会再打给他。

Sir: Do you want to leave message for him?
你想给他留口信吗？

Madam: When will he be back?
他什么时候回来？

Sir: I think he will be back in ten minutes.
我想他大概十分钟内回来。

Madam: I will call him later. Thanks!
我一会再打给他，谢谢！

Madam: Hello, this is Sanlitun Car Shop, can I help you?
你好，这是三里屯汽车店，有什么能为您效劳的吗？

Sir: This is Mr. Shi. I want to know your shop's working time.
我是史先生。我想问一下你们店的工作时间。

Madam: We are open from nine to five.
我们的工作时间从上午九点到下午五点。

Sir: Where is the location of your company?
你们公司在什么地方？

Madam: It's near the Workers' Stadium.
我们公司在工体附近。

3.2 Scene dialogue（英语场景会话篇）

3.2.1 Car received calls come（来电来人购车接待）

Madam:　　Hello, this is Sanlitun Car Shop. May I help you?

　　　　　你好，这里是三里屯汽车店，请问有什么可以帮您的吗？

Customer:　Hello, I'm Mr. Shi. I'm interested in the new Polo. Could you tell me the performance and price of this car?

　　　　　你好，我是史先生，我对你们的最新款Polo车感兴趣。我想问一下这款车的性能和价位？

Madam:　　You've made a good choice. We can definitely meet your demands. Can I make a suggestion?

　　　　　您真有眼力，我们肯定能满足您的要求。我能有个建议吗？

Customer:　Sure.

　　　　　当然可以。

Madam:　　If you have time, I want to pay you a visit for detailed explanations. In this way, you can have a better idea about this car. What do you think?

　　　　　如果您方便的话我想拜访您，向您详细地介绍一下。这样您就可以更清楚地了解这款车，您认为呢？

Customer:　It's OK. How long will it take?

　　　　　行，那详细地讲解需要多少时间啊？

Madam: Not more than one and a half hours. When will you be available?

不会超过一个半小时。您什么时候方便啊？

Customer: I prefer tomorrow afternoon.

明天下午方便。

Madam: Would 15:00 be all right?

那您认为三点钟怎么样？

Customer: It's okay.

好的。

Madam: Good. Could you leave me your phone number? I will visit you tomorrow afternoon. Thanks!

好，那您留一下您的电话，到时候我去拜访您，谢谢。

3.2.2 Regular maintenance
（定期维护）

Madam: Good morning. What can I do for you?

早上好，有什么需要我帮忙的地方吗？

Customer: I can't start my car, and I don't know the reason.

我的汽车不起动了，不知道是什么原因。

Madam: Have you tried more than once?

您多尝试几次了吗？

Customer: Yeah, I have, but failed to get it started.

是的，尝试了，但是还是不行啊。

Madam: What's your car and where is your location?

您开的是什么车啊，位置在哪里？

Customer: My car is a Toyota Corolla and I'm near the Dong Zhimen Bridge.

我的车是丰田卡罗拉，位置在东直门桥附近。

Madam: Okay, we will be there in 10 minutes. （after checking） Oh, something wrong with your car's engine and we'd better take your car back to our company to check.

好的，我们十分钟后赶到。（检查之后）哦，原来是汽车发动机出故障了，我们得拖回厂里检查。

Customer: Oh, that's all right.

哦，那好吧。

How to maintain the engine
如何维护发动机

Bad driving habits can let engine life shorter

坏的驾驶习惯会缩短发动机寿命

Here are some tips for you：

下面是给您的一些提示：

1. Driving only short trips without letting the engine to warm up fully

   如果没有热车就不要开太远

2. To prevent the engine from overheating, you must always keep the coolant level full

   必须始终保持有足够的冷却液，防止发动机过热

3. Use good fuel and oil and always keep the oil level full

   使用优质燃油和润滑油,并始终保持足够的油量

4. Change oil and oil filter on regular basis

   定期地更换机油和更换滤清器

5. Fix any minor engine problems on time

   发动机发生任何小故障都要及时修理

Reasons of engine overheats 发动机过热的原因

1. 缺乏冷却液	lack of coolant
2. 上下水管不良	faulty hose
3. 风扇皮带宽松	loose fan belt
4. 节温器损坏	defective thermostat
5. 冷却液通道闭塞	coolant passages blocked
6. 冷却风扇损坏	faulty cooling fan
7. 点火时间不当	ignition timing incorrect
8. 水泵损坏	faulty water pump
9. 汽缸垫损坏	faulty cylinder-head gasket

3.2.3 How to reduce emissions (如何减少废气排放)

David: Hi, it's been a long time. How are you recently?

你好,好久没有见了,你最近怎么样啊?

John: I'm okay. How about you?

我最近挺好的,你呢?

David: Business as usual. I heard that you want to buy a new car. Is that true?

我也还是老样子,听说你要买车,是吗?

John: Yeah. But after considering a series of issues, such as registration, insurance, maintenance and inspection, especially the environmental issue, I gave up that idea.

是啊，开始想买来着，后来考虑到车辆登记、保险与保养还有验车等一系列问题，尤其是环境问题，还是放弃这个想法了。

David: I didn't know that you are an environmentalist.

没有想到你还是名环保人士！

John: Of course I am! Now I carpool with my colleagues everyday. Promoting the idea of three or more passengers in a car can help reduce carbon emissions.

那当然！现在每天跟人拼车上下班呢。鼓励车辆搭乘3名或者更多的乘客以便减少碳排放。

David: That's a great idea. Because of the improvement of livelihood, many people can afford a car. Every year, there is a big rise in the total number of automobiles. That's a challenge for environmental protection and emission control.

你这个方法值得推广啊，现在人们的经济条件好了，很多人都能买得起车了，所以车辆每年增加的非常快，对环境和对废气的控制是个挑战呢。

John: Indeed, I think the government should come up with a series of methods to address this issue. Besides improving public transportation and conducting no-driving-day regulations, The government should also promote carpooling, build more non-driveways,

reduce the number of driveways and encourage people to use bicycle more. You have no idea how many lands those driveways and highways have occupied.

是啊，我认为政府应该出台一系列措施来应对这个问题。除了大力发展公共交通、限号行驶之外，还应该鼓励多人搭乘计划，多修非机动车道，少建机动车道，鼓励人们骑自行车。你不知道好多机动车道和高速路占了我们国家好多的土地资源呢。

David: Yeah, and I think car owners should pay for the roads they drive on and the oil they burned. The more you drive, the more you have to pay for environmental protection.

对的，我认为驾驶汽车的人还应该对他行驶的里程数和燃烧的汽油付费，如果你行驶的里程数越多，就应该多付治理环境的费用。

John: I agree. I heard that some people living in suburban areas drive to metro stations near their home and then go to work by metro.

是啊，听说现在有的住在郊区的人每天把车开到地铁附近的停车场，然后坐地铁去市里面上班。

David: I think the government should reward these people.

我认为政府对这样的人应该奖励啊。

John: I totally agree with you. It's time for me to go, see you later.

我也是这么认为的，我有事先走了，回见啊。

David: Okay. See you later.

好的，回见。

3.2.4 Traffic accident
（交通事故）

David: Did you hear that Toyota has received many complaints recently?

听说了吗，最近丰田汽车接到了好多投诉啊？

John: Yeah, I heard that car accidents in the US involving Toyota cars have caused many casualties.

是啊，听说了。听说驾驶丰田车造成的交通事故在美国发生很多起，造成很多人伤亡。

David: Do you know the cause?

你知道是由什么原因造成的吗？

John: I heard that it's something to do with the accelerator pedals, driver's floor mats and brakes.

听说是加速踏板、驾驶座脚垫和制动踏板等部件的缺陷造成的。

David: Oh, gosh, those are important safety parts for a car.

天哪，那可是汽车安全非常重要的部分啊！

John: Yeah, Last year, California highway patrol officer Mark Saylor and his three family members were killed. That was the worst accident happened that year involving a Toyota car.

是啊，听说最严重的一起事故是去年一名加利福尼亚州高速公路巡警 Mark Saylor 和他的三名家人由于丰田车本身的设计缺陷而丧生了。

David: Gosh, that's terrible!

天哪，真的是让人听起来太伤心了！

John: According to statistics, more than 100,000 people died in car accidents every year.

据统计，每年由于汽车的交通事故造成的死亡人数超过十万。

David: Oh, my God. It's hard to imagine!

天哪，太难以想象了！

Car accident glossary　汽车事故词汇表

automobile insurance	汽车保险	judgment	判决
best evidence	主要证据，最好的证据	lawyer	律师
case	案件	mistrial	无效审判
damage	损坏	petition	请愿
en banc	全体法官	record	记录
file	文件	settlement	解决
hearing	听证会	trial	审判，审讯
injure	伤害	verdict	判决书
		witness	证人

3.2.5 The recall of automotive products
（汽车产品的召回）

Amy: Did you hear the news about Toyota calling back those faulty cars?

你听到新闻了吗，说丰田公司在全球大规模召回有故障的车辆。

Peter: Yeah, I saw the news. Problems in those cars caused those accidents, not the drivers.

是的，是由于车辆本身的设计缺陷所引起的一系列事故，而不是司机的人为因素。

Amy: What do you think of this recall issued by Toyota?

你如何看待这次的召回？

Peter: Well, to safeguard customers' rights and interests, it's better to build a mature recall system.

我倒是认为为了保护消费者的权益，应该建立一套较为成熟的召回制度。

Amy: Really? I think they issued the recall due to defect products.

为什么这样说呢？我认为是它们的产品质量有问题，所以才把车召回。

Peter: Recall is a common in car industry. Every big car companies has such a record. There are tens of thousands components in a car. Nothing is perfect. So are the cars.

召回在汽车业界是家常便饭。世界上几乎任何一家成规模的汽车厂都有过召回产品的记录。几万个零件组成一辆汽车。金无足赤、人无完人，车也不可能完美得无懈可击。

Amy: But this time, Toyota didn't issue the recall until the problem was made public by media.

但是丰田的这次召回事件是被迫的，被媒体曝光之后才采取的行动。

Peter: Yeah, that's true. But history shows that great companies learn from their mistakes. I think Toyota will learn a lesson from this recall. You should admit your mistakes and correct them, and take full responsibility for your customers.

这倒是，不过历史证明很多大公司都是从他们的错误中吸取经验的，丰田公司通过这次召回事件应该学到教训了。要勇于知错就改，对客户采取认真负责的态度。

Amy: I totally agree.

我完全同意你的看法。

3.2.6　Car washing and waxing
（洗车及打蜡）

Dialogue

M: How are you, Madam. What can I do for you?

你好，女士，请问有什么可以帮你的吗？

C: I want to have the basic maintenance for my mini-cooper. I have driven it for 5000 kilometers.

我想给我的mini-cooper车做一下保养，它已经开了5000km了。

M: No problem. Please take a rest in our customer's lounge. I'll do it right away.

没有问题，请在我们的顾客休息室休息一下，我马上给您的车做保养。

C: Thank you.

谢谢。

(30 minutes later)

（三十分钟后）

M: Madam, the maintenance for your mini-cooper has already been finished. Our 4S shop can help you with wash and waxing.

女士，您的mini-cooper车已经保养好了，我们4S店还给您的车提供清洗和打蜡的业务。

C: You're so kind. Thanks, By the way, can you show me how to wash and wax my car?

你真是太好了,谢谢你!顺便问一下,你能告诉我如何清洗和打蜡吗?

M: Sure. Firstly, you must flush away the dust and sand on the surface of the car, otherwise you may scratch it.

没问题。首先您必须用水把车表面的浮尘和沙子清洗掉,那样的话车子将不会被划伤。

C: What should I use and how?

那我应该用什么洗并且怎么洗啊?

M: You can use a clean sponge with car detergent. Wash it up and down at first, and then backward and forward. Wash the wheels at last.

您可以用一块干净的海绵和汽车洗涤剂来洗车。首先要上下洗,然后前后洗。最后再来洗车轮。

C: And then?

那然后呢?

M: Use a special polish rag. If you use a common rag, its fluff will stick to the car surface.

用一块特殊的抛光布。因为如果用普通的布来擦车的话,布的绒毛就会附着在车的表面上。

C: Oh, I see. And the next step is waxing, right?

哦,我知道了。那么下一个步骤就是打蜡了吧?

M: Yeah. You can use different kinds of waxes for beautifying its body and leather seats. There are two kinds of waxes: hard wax and soft wax. Generally speaking, hard wax lasts longer.

是的，你可以用不同的蜡来美化车身和皮革座椅。车身蜡有两种：硬蜡和软蜡。一般来说硬蜡更持久一些。

C: When should I wax my car? What notice should I take?

什么时候打蜡？打蜡的时候我应该注意些什么呢？

M: You have to be sure that there is no dust on the car's surface. A thin layer of wax will do.

你最好确信当打蜡的时候，车的表面没有灰尘。为了保护车，打上一层薄薄的蜡就可以了。

C: Do I need to wait for the wax to dry?

我需要等到蜡干了才可以吗？

M: Yes. You'd better do it according to the manual.

对，给车打蜡最好根据使用说明来。

C: Thanks a lot.

非常感谢。

References
（参考文献）

[1] 丰田汽车公司. 丰田雅力士发动机1NZ-FE机械修理手册（英文版）[M]. 日本：丰田汽车公司，2016.

[2] 林振江. 汽车工业英文 [M]. 台北：全华图书股份有限公司，2015.

[3] How-do-all-electric-cars-work [DB/OL]. https://afdc.energy.gov/vehicles/，2019.

[4] 自动车公论社编辑部. 自动车整备士的英语 [M]. 东京：自动车公论社，2007.

[5] 中等职业学校职业英语教材编写组. 汽车英语 [M]. 北京：高等教育出版社，2006.